RIDE GUIDE:
Covered Bridges of Ohio

by Kurt Leib &
Steve Butterman

RIDE GUIDE Covered Bridges of Ohio
Copyright 1999 by Kurt Leib and Steve Butterman

Cover: *photo by Kurt Leib; design by Jean Sullivan*

Maps & Truss Illustrations: *Richard Widhu*

ISBN: 0-933855-16-8
Library of Congress Catalog Card Number: 99-67523

Also available:
Bed, Breakfast & Bike Mid-Atlantic
Bed, Breakfast & Bike Pacific Northwest
RIDE GUIDE New Jersey Mountain Biking
RIDE GUIDE North Jersey 2nd Edition
RIDE GUIDE Central Jersey 2nd Edition
RIDE GUIDE South Jersey 2nd Edition
RIDE GUIDE Mountain Biking in the New York Metro Area
RIDE GUIDE Hudson Valley New Paltz to Staten Island 2nd Edition
and
Happy Endings by Margaret Logan

Send for our catalog!

Published by

PRESS INC.

P.O. Box 156, Liberty Corner, New Jersey 07938

"Ride Guide" and "Bed, Breakfast and Bike" are trademarks of Anacus Press, Inc.

Printed in the United States of America

About the Authors

The authors of this book share some common passions. Both have logged literally thousands of miles plying the back roads of Ohio by bicycle. Both share a natural curiosity for things historical. This project was an opportunity to marry these interests by collaborating on a book highlighting Ohio's historic covered bridges by featuring them prominently in bicycle tours.

Steve Butterman began this project by conducting exhaustive research into many of the covered bridges featured in this book. He also did extensive field work laying out many of the routes contained in this *RIDE GUIDE*. Steve is an avid cyclist and novice historian now studying at The Ohio State University. This project never would have gotten off the ground without his vision.

Kurt Leib also has a penchant for cycling and spent many enjoyable hours riding some of the same roads featured in this *RIDE GUIDE* and stumbled upon a number of the covered bridges contained in this book before being asked to join the project. His writings on cycling have appeared in *Bike Midwest* magazine, a monthly publication that circulates in six Midwestern states, and has also spent over six years as a legislative correspondent covering the Ohio Statehouse. Kurt has a bachelor's degree in journalism from The Ohio State University. He now works for the Ohio Grocers Association in Columbus. Kurt lives in Powell with his wife, Nikki, and daughter Alexis.

Contents

Contents

Preface

It's been suggested that one should follow the path less traveled. That's certainly the case for the tours detailed in this *RIDE GUIDE*, each of which features a sampling of the historic covered bridges scattered throughout the Ohio countryside. Covered bridges are a truly distinctive part of Americana. While you could certainly cover the enclosed routes by automobile, the authors favor a mode of transportation that affords tourists the chance to slow down and enjoy the sights and sounds of the road: the bicycle. When you think about it, this is the best way to capture the spirit of the covered bridges, which in many instances were built around the same time the bicycle became a popular way of traveling short distances. And because these structures are often tucked away off the beaten track, they are a perfect destination for cyclists, who most often prefer areas with a lower volume of vehicle traffic.

But it's important to remember why the bridges exist in the first place. In the early to mid-19th century, many lives and possessions were lost by settlers trying to cross raging waters by foot, by horse, and on treacherous foot bridges. Numerous covered bridges, including some that are featured in this book, were erected specifically to provide a safer way to cross rivers and streams to avert these near-tragedies. The reason for covering wooden bridges is neither to grant shelter to travelers nor privacy for sweethearts (these structures have been nicknamed the Kissing Bridges), but to protect the bridge's framework from the elements, specifically rain. Wood actually survives the effects of salt better than either steel or concrete.

Wooden bridges were also popular in the heavily-forested eastern U.S. because timber was plentiful and close at hand, meaning durable wooden bridges could be constructed rapidly and inexpensively.

The first important decision in designing a new covered bridge was determining what type of truss design to use. A bridge's trusses are interlocking triangles that support the bridge and absorb the stress of vehicles passing over it, transferring the weight to the abutments (the foundations on the banks, typically constructed from limestone or sandstone quarried nearby). Each bridge has two trusses, one on either side; you can see a bridge's trusses from its interior. There are many different truss designs, and Ohio has the greatest variety still standing.

Each type of truss is described and illustrated in the Glossary of Bridge Terms, beginning on page 93. If you desire more information, visit a library or bookstore for other publications dedicated solely to covered bridges. I especially recommend *The Covered Bridges of Ohio* by Miriam Wood of the Ohio Historic Bridge Association. An educational and interesting book, it discusses all major truss types and their designers, renders the histories of Ohio's bridges past and present, and also has biographical sketches of local builders.

At one time, the young United States had well over 10,000 covered bridges; today, the number stands at about 700. Ohio itself was home to about 4,000 covered bridges and now has about 125, second among the states to Pennsylvania. Less than 50 still carry vehicle traffic. Most were constructed between 1829 and 1915, with about 75 percent of these covered bridges erected in the two decades following the Civil War.

In their heyday they could be compared to today's massive road-building projects, because bridges allowed hordes of settlers to expand into the Midwest. Covered bridges actually go much further back into antiquity. In Luzern, Switzerland, a covered bridge spanning the Reuss river is reputed to have been built in 1333. Another covered bridge over the Rhine River in Germany is said to have been built in 1685. The first covered bridge to be built in the U.S.—now long gone—was over the Schuykill River in Philadelphia in 1800. After that, covered bridge construction kept pace with new road construction. The bridge designers and builders were imported from Europe and were mainly immigrants from Germany, Switzerland, and Italy.

In the latter half of the 19th century, the burgeoning steel and iron industries influenced bridge design and construction. New steel and iron bridges gradually became favored for busier roads, relegating new covered bridge construction to the backroads, where most of the surviving ones now solemnly stand. Several great floods late last century and early this century, capped off by the devastating flood of 1913, sealed the fate of hundreds of Ohio covered bridges. For the most part, those that were destroyed were replaced by steel and iron structures. The heyday of Ohio's covered bridges had come to an end.

Of course, remaining covered bridges continue to be susceptible to flood damage, but those that remain are generally located in a manner to avoid floods. In fact, all but a handful of Ohio's remaining covered bridges survived that devastating 1913 flood. A number of other covered bridges met their demise because of the building of flood-control reservoirs in the middle part of this century. Strip mining in the southeastern region and truck drivers everywhere who ignore weight-limit signs have destroyed numerous other covered bridges.

One age-old threat to covered bridges that persists to this day is fire, specifically arson. As Steve researched Ohio's covered bridges for this book, he found that in recent years several old bridges that would otherwise have been included had succumbed to arson. Arson is now, and will remain, the primary threat to the remaining covered bridges.

Thankfully there are enlightened county engineers, protective local residents, bridge-activists within historical societies, and members of the Ohio Historic Bridge Association (OHBA) to counter those bent on destroying these magnificent structures. This book is dedicated in part to these enlightened citizens.

Starting in the 1960s, OHBA (then the Southern Ohio Covered Bridge Association) publicity campaigns helped increase public awareness and appreciation of covered bridges. OHBA members call themselves "Bridgers" (basically, meaning bridge-hunting fanatics) and do much to help protect the remaining historic bridges, be they covered, metal, concrete, or stone. Their activities include publicizing the bridges, persuading decision-makers to preserve and protect them, swapping stories about bridges and their builders, raising funds for needed renovations, and even descending en masse, scrub and paint brushes in hand, to clean up vandalized bridges.

As mentioned, only about a third of Ohio's covered bridges still carry regular traffic. Those that are no longer in service typically have either been moved to a new location, bypassed (meaning a new bridge has been built nearby and the road altered to cross over it), or simply "closed." Once, these actions often meant neglect and deterioration, but now these actions are mainly made for the sake of preserving these structures for future generations.

Often the relocated bridges are placed in scenic settings, such as in state or city parks; unfortunately, other "moved" bridges are taken to private property. This does not seem to be happening as often as it did a few decades ago. Small picnic areas surround some of the bypassed bridges that, though no longer carrying traffic, remain in their natural, original settings. A "closed" covered bridge no longer allows traffic on it; some closed bridges are on dead-end roads, others await either relocation or a bypass that will take traffic elsewhere. At press time, about a third of the covered bridges in this book are active, another third bypassed, and a third moved. Others are closed, with some routes beginning at the new home of a relocated bridge.

With this _RIDE GUIDE_, the authors hope to draw attention to and renew interest in Ohio's covered bridges in order to help save some of these magnificent and magical structures. Like anything else, these bridges are subject to the ravages of time, but also are threatened by vandals and often slated for demolition or replacement. While we have done everything we can to assure the accuracy of these routes prior to publication, it's a fact of life that covered bridges are destroyed or dismantled and relocated. This is why we strongly suggest that you use the information contained in the back of the book to contact area visitor's centers before making your trip. Also, if time warrants, drop a line to the Ohio Historical Bridge Association, 3155 Whitehead Road, Columbus, Ohio 43204.

The culture of cyclists includes subgroups like bike tourists, bike racers, bike commuters, and off-road bikers. You are about to join a new subgroup: bike bridgers. Enjoy your rural rides and enjoy your visits to these fine old structures.

The Parks/South Covered Bridge in Perry County was constructed across Painter Run in 1883. It features a multiple kingpost truss and is listed on the National Register of Historic Places.

Before You Go

This _RIDE GUIDE_ contains all the information you'll need for many years of cycling pleasure. Once you get a taste of the various routes contained in this book, you will find yourself returning year after year. If you need additional information about other local attractions and/or accommodations, about covered bridges, about bike travel in general, or about the condition of cycling roads between this book's routes and throughout the state, contact the sources listed on page 105.

In addition to all the information contained in this book, you'll need a suitable bike and some basic equipment before heading out on the open road. Generally, any mechanically-sound bike that fits properly is suitable for most of the routes covered in this publication. But if you are not accustomed to chugging up steep grades, such as those found on the routes in the southeastern region of the state, it may be a good idea to consult your local bike shop mechanic on the possibility of changing the gear ratios on your bike to take some of the sting off the steep hills you are likely to encounter. Sometimes, all it takes to produce a climbing machine is to swap out the larger front chain ring with one that contains fewer teeth. A mountain, hybrid, or cross bike may also be more comfortable on those routes that feature unpaved tracts of roadway.

Anticipated weather affects your choice of clothing. If you'll ride on a cool day—in mid-October, for instance, when the tree-top hues dramatically alter—you'll want to wear or at least take a pair of sweats/tights or a wind breaker, perhaps even full-fingered cotton gloves. In cool weather, layering clothes, especially on your upper body, works best for cycling because you can peel off layers as the day warms up. Personally, I recommend riding these loops during the warm, lush summertime (early or late summer to avoid excessive heat). Of course, summertime in Ohio can be full of surprises, including the sudden thunderstorm. To protect yourself from a good soaking, take along some simple raingear, at the least a packable hooded rainjacket that can be stashed in a back pocket. This may be enough to get you to shelter—like the next covered bridge! Speaking of summer, be sure to take along sufficient water and, on warm days, drink small amounts continually, even when you don't feel thirsty. The effects of dehydration can sneak up on even a highly-conditioned athlete.

You'll seldom be far from civilization, so by taking a mechanically sound bike you eliminate the need for an extensive repair kit. I would, however, at least take tire irons, a pump, a patch kit, even a spare tube. If you're not already familiar with it, practice replacing or patching a tube before you head out on the open road.

A few other items specifically recommended for these rides include a camera and film for photographing bridges, insect repellent for persistent summertime mosquitoes, and possibly some type of canine repellent for the chance encounter with a dog. By all means enjoy the peaceful surroundings on your forays into the country, but also be on the lookout for dogs, which can quickly dart out and startle riders.

Over the years, I have had a few run-ins with dogs, but fortunately I have been able to sprint away to the end of the dog's territory, which is where they will generally give up the chase. Some riders like to take along dog repellent, which is effective at close range. Another effective lower-tech solution is right in front of you: a water bottle. A quick squirt in the face of an oncoming dog will startle it enough to give most cyclists a chance to make a run for it.

Be the problem a dog, a vehicle, or anything else, if you take a spill an approved, ANSI- or Snell-rated helmet can save your health, or even your life. A good helmet should have a comfortable fit and weigh very little. While professional cyclists in the European peloton often prefer to go helmet-free, you should wear one at all times. Even with a helmet and dog-strategy, you can further increase your safety by maximizing your visibility, obeying traffic laws, and practicing safe riding techniques. Wearing brightly-colored clothing can increase visibility, and be sure your bicycle is equipped with reflectors. If there is a possibility your wandering may keep you out after dark, Ohio law requires your bike to have a headlamp and tail light.

In Ohio, bicyclists have the same rights and responsibilities on the road as motor vehicles, with the exception that bikes must stay on the far right side of the road when in traffic. When riding with others, you are permitted to ride two abreast. Whenever possible, use hand signals to show your intent to turn, slow down or stop as a courtesy to drivers and other riders in a group. Otherwise, do not ride timidly and do not consider yourself a second-class citizen on the road.

Fortunately, the vast majority of the roads on these rides have little traffic. Those few roads subject to moderate or heavier traffic will be identified in the route description.

Finally, the existence and locations of covered bridges can change. Most of the covered bridges in this *RIDE GUIDE* are valued and protected as historic landmarks, but they can still fall victim to vandals, arson, and overloaded vehicles, or may simply be moved to a new location for the sake of preservation. For example, a covered bridge in southern Ohio was washed away during the horrendous floods that swept through the region in the spring of 1997. So, it may be a good idea to contact the local chamber of commerce for any updates. Happy cycling.

How To Use This Book

Each chapter in this *RIDE GUIDE* follows a specific format. Familiarizing yourself with the layout of this book before you ride will help you get the most enjoyment out of your chosen route.

The ride title contains either the starting point or the destination for the trip. All of the routes are loops so that they return the rider to the starting point. Some include short cuts, and others have out-and-back spurs that take you to additional points of interest.

Mileage is only one factor to consider in selecting a route, but it is an important consideration. If you've never cycle-toured before, it is probably best to start with a mileage under 25. Don't let these numbers intimidate you—even beginners can tool along at 12 mph or better on flat roads. And if you have the whole day or even half a day, you won't have to push yourself to finish a 25-mile ride, even if it has some hills.

Other factors to consider have a listing with each ride. They are **terrain, road conditions, traffic,** and **points of interest.**

Terrain is probably the most important consideration for most riders. Ohio is generally considered flat, but the terrain actually varies quite a bit. New riders might consider "gently rolling" sections rather hilly, while the experienced rider won't even notice the uphills. After completing some of the shorter routes in *RIDE GUIDE*, most riders will develop endurance and strength in their legs so they will be ready to challenge the longer rides.

Traffic is an important consideration, especially when riding on weekdays. Roads that are a cyclist's paradise most of the time can become harrowing at rush hour. In tourist areas, like the Logan-Indian Lake ride, traffic is heaviest on weekends.

Road Conditions are generally good for all of the routes in this book, except for a few rough stretches where noted. Since many of the remaining covered bridges are off the beaten trail, some routes include brief stretches of dirt road or rideable gravel that is best suited to a hybrid or mountain bike.

Points of Interest suggests where to get off your bike and pull out the camera or spread a picnic blanket. Of course, every ride features a handful of covered bridges, but there are monuments, historic sites, and beautiful scenery to take in, as well.

Directions to Starting Point gives driving instructions to reach the beginning of each route. Some of these starting points may be within riding distance of a vacation spot, but others are quite a distance from the usual motels.

Cue Sheets list every turn and point of interest along the route. Riders should read the whole cue sheet before starting a ride. Some cyclists have a plastic envelope on their handlebar bags to keep the cue sheet in view while riding. On the cue sheets, **Pt.-Pt.** indicates the mileage between turns or points of interest. **Cume**, short for cumulative, gives total mileage from the start. Abbreviations in the **Turn** column are:

L	Left
R	Right
S	Straight
BL	Bear Left
BR	Bear Right
SL	Sharp Left
SR	Sharp Right

Street/Landmark prints the name of the street for the route in **boldface**. A (T) is an intersection where the road ends and the route goes either right or left.

Maps provide the general course of the ride. They show cross streets and some shortcuts. It is a good idea to have a local map along, too, as roads can change, and street signs can disappear.

The State Road Covered Bridge in Ashtabula County is not included in any of the routes in this book, but is worth a side trip. The ceremony that marked the opening of this bridge in 1983 was the forerunner of the Ashtabula County Covered Bridge Festival. Featuring a Town Lattice truss design, the 152-foot structure contains 97,000 feet of southern pine and oak. Ashtabula County continues to construct new covered bridges, opening the Netcher Road Covered Bridge in 1999.

Ride Starting Points

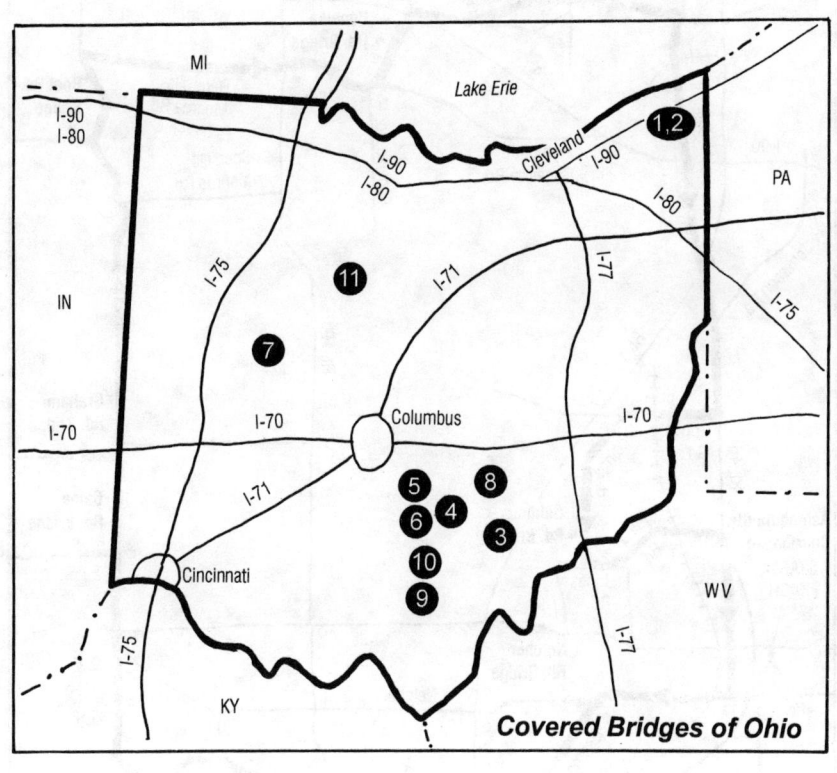

Covered Bridges of Ohio

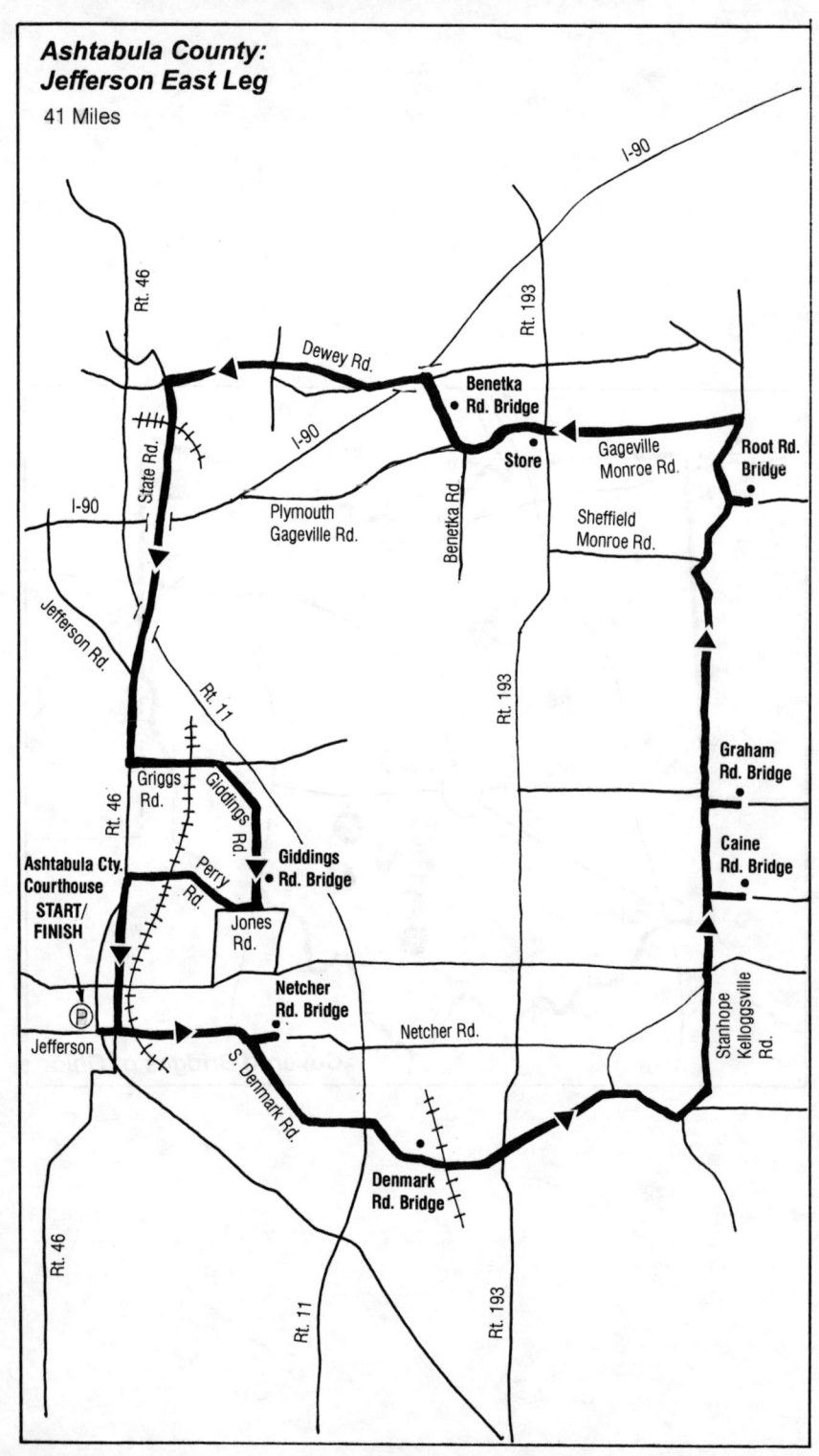

Ashtabula County: Jefferson East Leg— 41 miles

Terrain: Mainly flat, with some rolling hills.

Road Conditions: Generally very well maintained paved roads, with the exception of some brief sections of gravel road.

Traffic: Very light, even on the weekends.

Points of Interest: Netcher Road Covered Bridge, South Denmark Road Covered Bridge, Caine Road Covered Bridge, Graham Road Covered Bridge, Root Road Covered Bridge, Benetka Road Covered Bridge, Giddings Road Covered Bridge.

Situated in the extreme northeast corner of Ohio, Ashtabula County has a long history when it comes to covered bridges. The county is home to a total of 16 covered bridges of various types and is likely the only area in the state where *new* covered bridges are being constructed. The **Netcher Road Covered Bridge**, the first stop on the eastern leg of Ashtabula County, was in the final stages of construction during my visit on a beautiful early summer day. Construction on this bridge spanning Mill Creek measures 110 feet long and features a timber arch with inverted Haupt walls. Work on this "Neo Victorian" bridge began in 1998 thanks to funding from the Ohio Department of Transportation.

Residents of Ashtabula County treasure their covered bridges. In fact, the area celebrates these wonderful structures every year during the Ashtabula County Covered Bridge Festival held in Jefferson, which is the jumping off point for both routes in this book. The festival is held during the second full weekend in October at the Ashtabula County Fairgrounds and is timed to coincide with the peak of the brilliant fall foliage. The festival features parades, arts and crafts demonstrations, antique cars and engines, and draft horse pulls. There are also guided van tours of area covered bridges as well as self-guided tours of all 16 bridges. The driving tour totals 135 miles, but for the purposes of this book, two very manageable bike routes have been carved out. Both of these tours can be completed in one day. On the eastern loop you will visit a total of seven covered bridges. In fact, there are signs of covered bridges everywhere you look. One bridge, originally constructed in 1862, has been moved and reconstructed for use as the Covered Bridge Pizza Parlor—you can dine right inside the old bridge!

Though things are a little more relaxed in Ashtabula County, there are enough area attractions and amenities to please anyone. Many Ohio wineries are located in the area and the vineyards can be seen from the roadside along the bike route. Most wineries offer tours, tastings and other special events year round, in addition to fine dining. Geneva-on-the-Lake, Ohio's first summer resort, is located on the shores of Lake Erie at the northern end of Ashtabula County.

Starting out at the Ashtabula County Courthouse in Jefferson, you'll head east out of town and quickly encounter the **Netcher Road Covered Bridge** mentioned earlier. During construction this bridge was not passable, but it's a beautiful structure that will stand up to traffic for years to come. A short distance down the road is the **South Denmark Road Covered Bridge**. Originally built in 1868, this Town lattice bridge spans Mill Creek. Measuring 80 feet in length, it was bypassed in 1975 but is easy to get to by bicycle. In fact, you can ride through this structure, but use caution—thin bicycle tires can easily drop into the spaces between the planks. You won't want to ruin a wheel because there is a lot left to see on this magnificent route.

About six miles down the road is the **Caine Road Covered Bridge**. This Pratt Truss bridge was erected in 1986 over the west branch of the Ashtabula River to mark the county's 175th Anniversary. At 96 feet long, this is one of the larger covered bridges in the area and is open to vehicle traffic. Just over a mile away sits the **Graham Road Covered Bridge**, which contains pieces from another bridge that was washed out during a flood in 1913. It stands in a small park on the south side of the road and provides a quiet and inviting resting place for cyclists.

About four miles further down Stanhope Kelloggsville Road sits the **Root Road Covered Bridge**. The 97-foot Town Lattice structure was originally built in 1868 over the Ashtabula River. A center concrete pier and new girders were added for support during an overhaul started in 1982.

The next stop on this tour is the **Benetka Road Covered Bridge,** built around 1900 to traverse the Ashtabula River. This 115-foot Town lattice bridge was renovated in 1985 with the addition of a laminated arch that runs the entire length of the bridge. During the return leg of this loop riders cross the **Giddings Road Covered Bridge**, a Pratt Truss structure measuring 104 feet in length. It was erected in 1995 using funds obtained from the Ohio Department of Transportation.

It is definitely worth the drive to see the diverse array of covered bridges available on this route. But the real benefit is the low traffic volume on the roads in the area.

Directions to the Starting Point: Jefferson is located in the heart of Ashtabula County and can be easily accessed from Interstate 90 by taking Route 46 south into town. The Ashtabula County Courthouse is located on Jefferson Street in downtown Jefferson. Turn right and the parking lot entrance is located behind the building near the Sheriff's Office. Public parking is available only on the weekends at the courthouse. During the week, parking spots downtown are reportedly at a premium.

Pt.-Pt.	Cume	Turn	Street/Landmark
0.0	0.0	**L**	Exit **Ashtabula County Courthouse** parking lot.
0.1	0.1	**S**	Stop light. Cross Rte. 46
0.3	0.4	**S**	Stop light.
0.1	0.5	**S**	Railroad crossing. *Be careful* over these uneven tracks!
1.4	1.9	**R**	Turn onto **South Denmark Rd.**

Pt.-Pt.	Cume	Turn	Street/Landmark
0.1	2.0	**L**	**Netcher Road Covered Bridge** is on the left. Road temporarily bypassed during construction. Continue **straight** on **Denmark Rd.**
1.3	3.3	**BL**	Left curve in road.
0.5	3.8	**S**	Cross over SR 11 overpass.
1.0	4.8	**BR**	**Denmark Road Covered Bridge** can be seen from the road, but it has been bypassed. The bridge is open to bicycle traffic, but use *extreme caution* because tires can fall into gaps in the planks.
0.0	4.8	**S**	Return to **Denmark Rd**. and continue straight.
0.4	5.2	**S**	Another railroad crossing. *Exercise caution!*
0.8	6.0	**S**	At stop sign, cross Rte. 193.
2.5	8.5	**L**	At "T" intersection, turn left onto **Stanhope Kelloggsville Rd.**
2.0	10.5	**S**	Continue straight on **Stanhope Kelloggsville Rd.**
0.9	11.4	**R**	Turn onto **Caine Rd.** *Caution:* gravel road!
0.4	11.8	**S**	Encounter **Caine Road Covered Bridge**
0.4	12.2	**S**	Backtrack on **Caine Rd.** returning to **Stanhope Kelloggsville Rd.**
0.0	12.2	**R**	Turn right onto **Stanhope Kelloggsville Rd.**
1.2	13.4	**R**	Turn onto **Graham Rd.**
0.2	13.6	**S**	Encounter **Graham Road Covered Bridge**. Turn around and head back to **Stanhope Kelloggsville Rd.**
0.2	13.8	**R**	Turn right onto **Stanhope Kelloggsville Rd.**
2.3	16.1	**BL**	Left curve in road.
0.3	16.4	**BR**	Right-hand curve in road.
0.3	16.7	**S**	Pass Sheffield Monroe Rd. on your left.
1.8	18.5	**BR**	**Root Road Covered Bridge**, now bypassed, but well maintained. Return to **Stanhope Kelloggsville Rd.**

Pt.-Pt.	Cume	Turn	Street/Landmark
1.1	19.6	L	Turn left onto **Gageville Monroe Rd.** There are several small hills to contend with.
2.5	22.1	S	At stop sign, continue straight near the **Gageville Country Store**. Now on **Plymouth-Gageville Rd.**
0.6	22.7	S	Encounter steep hill.
0.5	23.2	R	Turn onto **Benetka Rd.**
0.7	23.9	S	**Benetka Road Covered Bridge**. Continue straight.
0.1	24.0	S	Steep hill.
0.3	24.3	L	At the stop sign, turn left on **Dewey Rd.**
0.3	24.6	S	Cross over I-90 overpass.
0.5	25.1	BR	Right curve.
0.9	26.0	S	Steep hill. *Caution*: no shoulder through this area.
3.0	29.0	L	At stop sign, turn left onto **State Rd.**
0.4	29.4	S	Use care when crossing railroad tracks.
0.7	30.1	S	Continue straight at stop sign.
0.5	30.6	S	Cross over I-90.
1.3	31.9	S	Cross over SR 11
0.5	32.4	S	Pass Jefferson Rd. on your right.
1.3	33.7	L	Turn left onto **Griggs Rd.**
0.8	34.5	S	Cross railroad tracks *carefully!*
0.5	35.0	R	Turn right on **Giddings Rd.**
0.6	35.6	S	Road turns to gravel, but still rideable.
1.0	36.6	S	Pavement begins. Encounter the **Giddings Road Covered Bridge**
0.1	36.7	S	Gravel begins again.
0.3	37.0	R	At stop sign, turn right onto **Jones Rd.**
0.2	37.2	R	Turn right onto **Perry Rd.**
1.5	38.7	L	Turn onto **Rte. 46**. Traffic can be heavy at times.
1.6	40.3	S	Straight up hill.
0.4	40.7	S	Proceed straight at the flashing light.
0.2	40.9	R	At stop light, turn right onto **Jefferson St.**
0.1	41.0	R	Turn into **Ashtabula County Courthouse** parking lot. End of route.

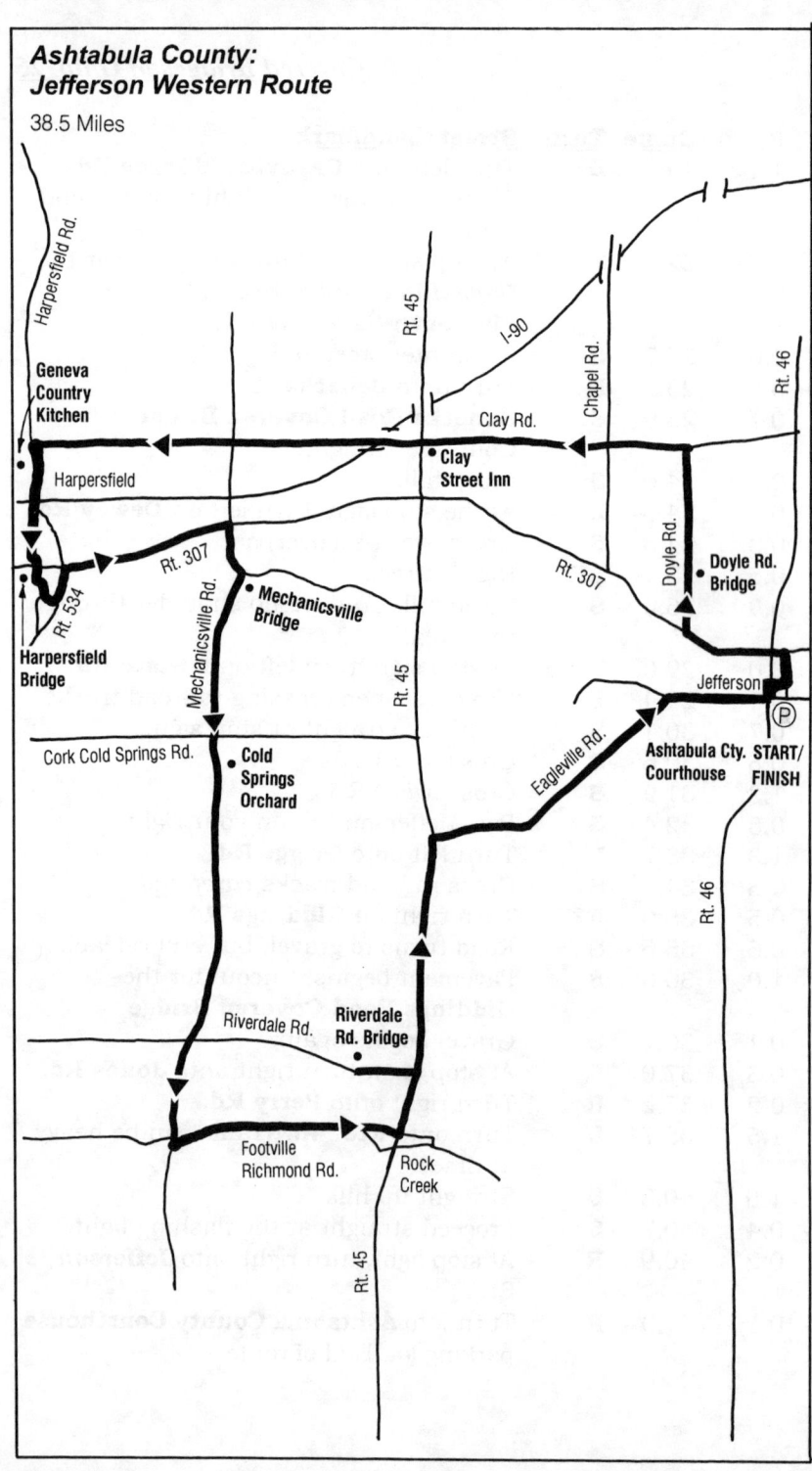

Ashtabula County: Jefferson Western Route— 38.5 miles

Terrain: Gently rolling, with some steep climbs.

Road Conditions: Well maintained paved roads, with the exception of one stretch of gravel road.

Traffic: Light to non-existent.

Points of Interest: Doyle Road Covered Bridge, Harpersfield Covered Bridge, Mechanicsville Covered Bridge, Riverdale Road Covered Bridge.

Though fewer bridges are visited on this route than on the eastern leg of Ashtabula County, this western route certainly has one of Ohio's most impressive covered bridges, the **Harpersfield Covered Bridge**. But there is also one important drawback to this loop: a long stretch of gravel begins just after the **Doyle Road Covered Bridge**, which is the first stop on this tour. Because of this, a mountain bike is recommended for getting through this section of road and the rest of the route in comfort.

All of the covered bridges in the area have been painstakingly protected or restored. The Doyle Road Covered Bridge is no exception. Located about 2 miles outside Jefferson, this 84-foot-long structure was erected in 1876 over Mill Creek and renovated in 1987.

The Harpersfield Covered Bridge is the longest covered bridge in Ohio at a stunning 234 feet in length. This double span Howe Truss bridge was originally constructed in 1868 and is listed in the National Register of Historic Places. The setting can't be beat for its beauty, because the bridge sits in the County Metro Park and offers the perfect place for a picnic lunch. Like many other covered bridges in the area, this structure was damaged by the flood of 1913, which washed away soil at the north end of the bridge, thereby changing the river channel. A steel bridge was built and attached to the covered bridge where the old bank was eroded away by the flood. During an overhaul of the bridge in the early 1990s, a pedestrian walkway was added.

After stopping at the Harpersfield Covered Bridge, riders will encounter the area's other notable covered bridge. The **Mechanicsville Road Covered Bridge** has the distinction of being Ashtabula County's longest single span covered bridge at 154 feet. Built over the Grand River in 1867, this is believed to be the oldest covered bridge in the county. Now closed to vehicle traffic, preservationists have set their sights on restoring this magnificent structure soon.

Heading through the village of Rock Creek, look for the stunning hand-painted mural of a covered bridge on the side of the 3Cs Grocery Store. It's just one more example of the pride local residents have for the covered bridges scattered around Ashtabula County.

Directions to Starting Point: Jefferson is located in the heart of Ashtabula County and can be easily accessed from Interstate 90 by taking Route 46 south into town. The Ashtabula County Courthouse is located on Jefferson Street in downtown Jefferson. Turn right and the parking lot entrance is located behind the building near the Sheriff's Office. Public parking is available only on the weekends at the courthouse. During the week, parking spots downtown are reportedly at a premium.

Pt.-Pt.	Cume	Turn	Street/Landmark
0.0	0.0	L	Exit from **Ashtabula County Courthouse** by turning left onto **Jefferson St.**
0.1	0.1	L	Turn left onto **Rte. 46** at stop light.
0.5	0.6	L	Turn left onto **Rte. 307** at intersection.
1.2	1.8	R	Turn right onto **Doyle Rd.**
0.9	2.7	S	Encounter **Doyle Road Covered Bridge**.
0.0	2.7	S	Gravel begins just past bridge.
1.4	4.1	L	Turn left onto **Clay Rd.**

Pt.-Pt.	Cume	Turn	Street/Landmark
1.0	5.1	**S**	Pass Chapel Road.
2.4	7.5	**S**	**Clay Street Inn** on left (food and drink available). At stop sign, go straight crossing Rte. 45.
0.4	7.9	**S**	Cross over Interstate 90. *Caution:* rough road.
2.0	9.9	**S**	Road becomes smooth again.
1.5	11.4	**S**	Wine country scene appears.
0.9	12.3	**L**	Turn left onto **Harpersfield Rd**. *Caution:* heavy traffic at times.
0.1	12.4	**S**	Enter **Harpersfield**.
0.7	13.1	**S**	**Geneva Country Kitchen** (food/drink) on the right side.
0.1	13.2	**S**	Cross over I-90.
0.1	13.3	**BR**	Take right fork in the road.
0.5	13.8	**S**	Go straight at stop sign.
0.1	13.9	**SL**	Sharp left hand turn.
0.1	14.0	**S**	**Harpersfield Covered Bridge.** The park has a snack shop for food and/or refreshments.
0.3	14.3	**L**	Turn left at the intersection. (Covered Bridge Driving Tour sign posted)
0.5	14.8	**L**	Turn onto **Rt. 534**. Can be busy with traffic.
1.0	15.8	**R**	Turn right onto **Rt. 307**.
2.3	18.1	**R**	Turn right onto **Mechanicsville Rd**. A lovely tree-lined road leads to the **Mechanicsville Covered Bridge**.
0.1	18.2	**S**	Encounter a steep hill.
1.8	20.0	**S**	At stop sign, continue straight by crossing Cork Cold Springs Rd.
0.5	20.5	**S**	**Cold Springs Orchard** on the left.
2.6	23.1	**S**	Right-hand curve.
2.2	25.3	**L**	Turn onto **Footville-Richmond Rd**.
2.7	28.0	**S**	Enter the village of **Rock Creek**.
0.2	28.2	**L**	Turn left onto **Rte. 45**. Look for the **mural of the covered bridge** on the side of a grocery store.

Pt.-Pt.	Cume	Turn	Street/Landmark
0.9	29.1	**L**	Turn onto **Riverdale Rd**.
0.8	29.9	**S**	**Riverdale Road Covered Bridge.** Relax in a small clearing just past the bridge.
0.8	30.7	**L**	Backtrack to **Rte. 45**.
2.9	33.6	**R**	Turn onto **Eagleville Rd**.
3.6	37.2	**R**	Right turn.
0.3	37.5	**S**	Enter village of **Jefferson**.
0.5	38.0	**S**	At stop light, continue straight.
0.5	38.5	**L**	Turn into **Ashtabula County Courthouse** parking lot. End of route.

Ashtabula County's Doyle Road Covered Bridge features a Town truss and an 84-foot span over Mill Creek. It was constructed in 1876.

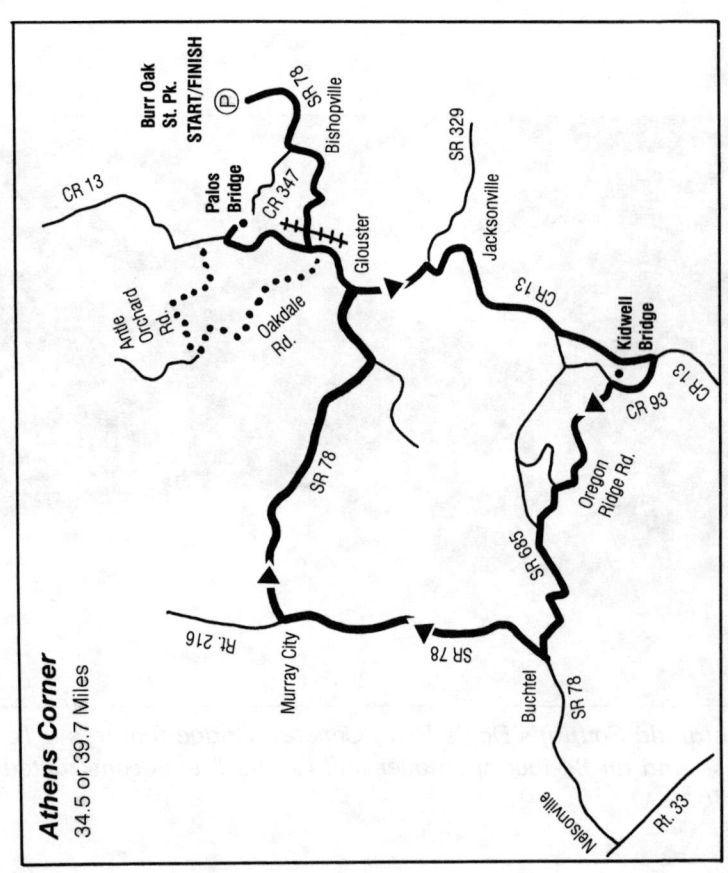

Athens Corner
34.5 or 39.7 Miles

Athens Corner—34.5 or 39.7 miles

Terrain: Very rolling, with some tough uphill climbs.

Road Conditions: All roads are paved and well-maintained, though an alternate loop is heavy gravel with some patches of pavement best suited for a mountain bike.

Traffic: Moderate to non-existent depending on the time of year. Vehicle traffic on State Route 78 can be rather heavy and the shoulder is narrow in places.

Points of Interest: Burr Oak State Park; Palos Covered Bridge; Kidwell Covered Bridge.

This route is situated in the extreme northeast corner of Athens County and actually dips into neighboring counties during the loop that begins and ends at the Burr Oak State Park Lodge. Because this tour is among the hardest to reach by vehicle, it makes sense to drive in on a Friday evening and stay over at the lodge to get an early start in the morning. This is why the start and finish are in the lodge parking lot. Believe me when I say you will probably want some extra time to complete this difficult figure-eight shaped loop, but the scenery makes it all worthwhile. The roads afford some splendid vistas overlooking lush valleys, and if you happen to catch this area in the fall it literally explodes with color.

Athens County has a rich history, and was one of the first areas to be settled in the days before Ohio won statehood. Home to Ohio University, one of the oldest land grant colleges in the nation, the county was created in 1805 by an act of the state legislature. Athens County was originally formed from land taken out of Washington County, Ohio's original county, where the state's first settlement—Marietta—is located. Some territory from the original Athens County was lost to the adjacent counties of Hocking, Jackson, Meigs, Morgan, and Vinton, shrinking the county to its present size of 484 square miles.

This tour visits two of the three covered bridges in Athens County, including the Palos and Kidwell covered bridges. Both are listed on the National Register of Historic Places. The **Palos Covered Bridge** spans Sunday Creek. Legend has it this creek got its name from an adventurous band of hunters who were out on an expedition. Instead of following the river where the ground was swampy, the party crossed the hills and camped near a creek on Saturday, staying in the area the next day, hence the name Sunday Creek. The Palos Covered Bridge is still very much in use and looks to be able to handle vehicle traffic for the foreseeable future. Though local artists have added their graffiti to the bridge, it appears solid. Exercise caution when crossing this bridge, because vehicle traffic can sneak up pretty quickly.

The **Kidwell Covered Bridge** is no longer open to traffic and is now closed. It sits just off County Route 93. Built in 1880, this is one of the older covered bridges still standing, although it has started to lean a bit to the right. The area is also overgrown with weeds and other vegetation. Be careful, because on the day I visited the site there were some mud wasp nests in the ceiling. I didn't bother to stay long enough to see if they were active!

The route snakes from Burr Oak, into Glouster, Jacksonville, out to Buchtel· and back to Burr Oak by way of Glouster. The Burr Oak Lodge has 60 guest rooms and 30 fully-furnished, two-bedroom cabins. There is also a full-service dining room open for breakfast, lunch and dinner. The lodge also has an indoor swimming pool for a refreshing dip at the end of a long day's ride. There are also miles of hiking trails, tennis, basketball, and fishing in Burr Oak Lake. For reservations call 1-800-AT-A-PARK. For more information call the lodge at (740) 767-2112.

There is an alternate loop built into this route just past Palos Covered Bridge that is not for the faint of heart. It travels straight up a road layered with heavy gravel that makes for slow going, even for a mountain bike. The good news is there are some patches of pavement that can help you reach the top of this steep grade. Those that withstand the test in the early going are benefited with a mainly downhill ride into the outskirts of Glouster before going on to the Kidwell Covered Bridge.

Directions to the starting point: The route begins and ends at the parking lot of the Burr Oak State Park Lodge. The easiest way to get to the lodge is to take U.S. Route 33 to Nelsonville and turn onto State Route 78 and follow it directly to the entrance to Burr Oak State Park outside Glouster.

Pt.-Pt.	Cume	Turn	Street/Landmark
0.0	0.0	S	Parking lot of **Burr Oak State Park Lodge**
0.4	0.4	R	Turn right at state park office
0.3	0.7	R	**SR 78**
0.2	0.9	SL	Sharp left turn
1.5	2.4	S	Enter **Bishopville**
1.2	3.6	BR	Sharp turn, steep downhill
0.8	4.4	S	Beautiful home on hillside
0.2	4.6	S	Railroad crossing—*use care!*
0.2	4.8	R	**CR 13**
1.3	6.1	R	**CR 347**
0.1	6.2	S	Encounter **Palos Covered Bridge**
0.1	6.3	S	Backtrack on **CR 347** to **CR 13**

(Alternate section begins)

0.0	0.0	R	**CR 13**
0.2	0.2	L	**Antle Orchard Rd.** (heavy gravel/steep hill)
0.8	1.0	S	Pavement begins!
0.3	1.3	S	Back to gravel
0.5	1.8	S	Brief patch of pavement
0.2	2.0	L	Turn onto **Oakdale Rd.** at stop sign
0.5	2.5	BR	Cross bridge
1.3	3.8	BL	Sweeping left turn
0.4	4.2	S	Enter **Glouster**
0.9	5.1	L	At stop sign turn onto SR 78
0.1	5.2	R	**CR 13** Rejoin route at mile 7.6.

Pt.Pt.-Pt.	Cume	Turn	Street/Landmark
			(If skipping loop up Antle Orchard Rd., pick up here)
1.3	7.6	**S**	Backtrack on **CR 13** to junction of SR 78
0.1	7.7	**S**	Enter **Glouster**
0.8	8.5	**BL**	Downtown (food, drink available)
0.2	8.7	**S**	Stop light. Straight on **CR 13**
0.2	8.9	**S**	**Glouster Memorial Park** on right
0.1	9.0	**S**	**Korea-Vietnam Memorial** on right
1.2	10.2	**S**	Enter **Jacksonville**
3.5	13.7	**R**	Turn onto **CR 93**
0.5	14.2	**S**	Cross bridge
0.8	15.0	**S**	Encounter **Kidwell Covered Bridge**, built in 1880. Continue on **CR 93**
0.3	15.3	**BL**	Keep left at fork in the road. Climb hill
0.6	15.9	**S**	Cross bridge, white church on the left
1.7	17.6	**S**	Steep uphill
1.9	19.5	**S**	Enter **Buchtel**
0.2	19.7	**BL**	Keep left at intersection
0.1	19.8	**R**	At stop sign turn right onto **SR 78**
0.3	20.1	**S**	Enter Hocking Co. sign.
2.8	22.9	**S**	Enter **Murray City**
0.3	23.2	**SR**	Sharp right turn
0.1	23.3	**SL**	Sharp left turn
0.3	23.6	**S**	Carry out on left for food and drink
0.1	23.7	**R**	Turn at stop sign, bear **left** immediately at church.
2.5	26.2	**S**	Cross bridge
1.4	27.6	**S**	Enter **Glouster**
1.1	28.7	**S**	Pass Oakdale (end of alternate loop)
0.1	28.8	**L**	Turn at stop light
0.2	29.0	**BR**	Right turn (Kroger on right hand side)
0.7	29.7	**BR**	Keep right on **SR 78**
0.2	29.9	**S**	Railroad crossing—*careful!*
1.0	30.9	**BL**	Steep left turn
0.4	31.3	**BR**	Enter **Bishopville**, keep right
2.3	33.6	**BR**	Sharp right turn
0.2	33.8	**L**	Lodge entrance

Pt.-Pt.	**Cume**	**Turn**	**Street/Landmark**
0.3	34.1	**L**	Turn at stop sign
0.4	34.5	**S**	Enter lodge parking lot. End of ride.

The Zeller/ Smith Covered Bridge was built across Sycamore Creek south of Pickerington in 1891. In 1986, the bridge was moved upstream into a town park, where it still spans Sycamore Creek as part of a bike path.

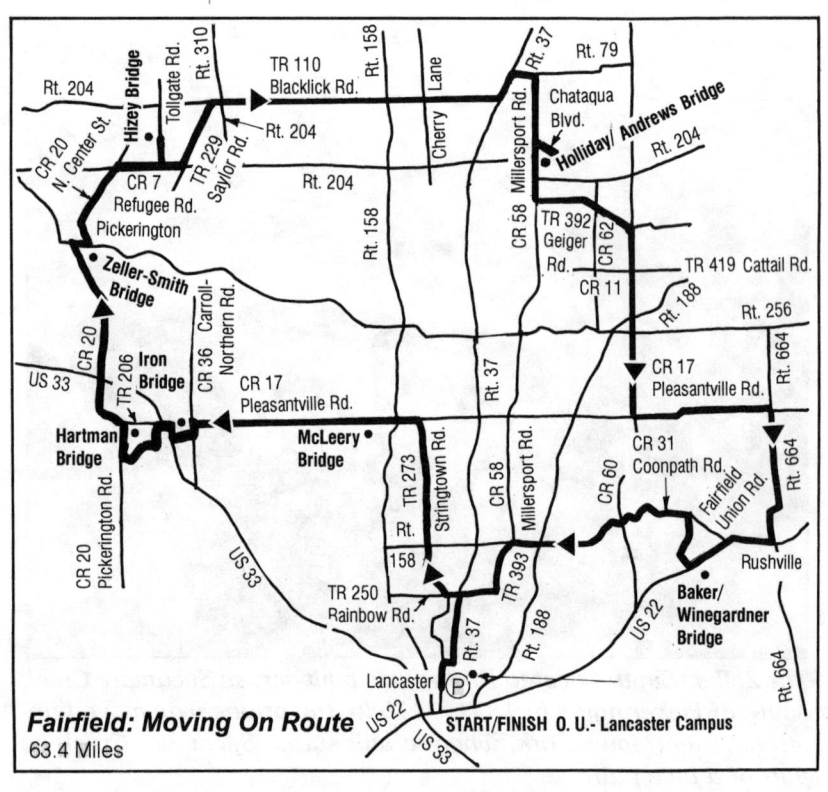

Fairfield: Moving On Route
63.4 Miles

START/FINISH O. U.- Lancaster Campus

Fairfield: Moving On Route—63.4 miles

Terrain: Mostly flat to mildly rolling, with several modest hills.

Road Conditions: Generally excellent and all paved except several very short sections of rideable gravel near the bridges.

Traffic: Light on the backroads and light-to-moderate near several small towns. Busier and faster traffic on SR 37 and US 22,but you are only on these briefly and both have good shoulders.

Points of Interest: John Bright #2 Covered Bridge; McLeery Covered Bridge; Hartman Covered Bridge in Lockville Park; Zeller/Smith Covered Bridge; (Optional) Hizey Covered Bridge; Holliday/Andrews Covered Bridge; Baker/Winegardner Covered Bridge.

Among Ohio's surviving covered bridges, about a third of them have been moved to new locations. This route touches seven of these relocated bridges, giving you a chance to sample the various ways that a covered bridge can be moved and preserved and to see for yourself how most relocations can preserve a bridge's charm and dignity while, unfortunately, some do not. Typical places for relocating a bridge include town parks, fairgrounds, campuses, and private property. This route includes examples of each. Generally, all have been relocated to fairly appealing new locations with the exception of the one at the Millersport Corn Festival Grounds. One repositioned bridge fairly close to this route's starting point is in such an unappealing location that the authors decided not to include it—the Roley School/Basil Canal Bridge, which sits forlornly just inside the main gate of the County Fairgrounds on North Broad Street in Lancaster.

Two of this route's relocated covered bridges (one of them optional) sit on private property; they both retain their charm and are both well maintained, but we hope that any additional covered bridges that have to be moved get moved to public property. Over a dozen of Ohio's covered bridges now sit on private property, and two other routes in this book will pass by one because they were on/near a route anyway. Always request the property owners' permission before examining these bridges up close.

Try not to let the length of this route intimidate you. The roads are smooth and often fairly level. Also, you'll pass through several small towns where you can replenish supplies as needed, and several of this route's bridge locations make excellent spots for a picnic. The route begins at the Ohio University branch campus in northern Lancaster. Settled in 1800, Lancaster contains several points of historical interest, including "Square 13," a National Historic District of 19th-century homes near downtown.

This route begins on the town's northern edge because of Lancaster's busy automotive traffic, but if you are interested in exploring the town, the County Visitors Bureau (see page 105) can send you any necessary information. On the O.U. campus is the very interesting and nicely relocated **John Bright #2 Covered Bridge**. This is one of only two covered bridges in the U.S. built with an inverted bowstring design. The other is the Germantown Bridge in Montgomery County, but the John Bright #2 differs in that it also has a Burr Arch, making for an unusual, pleasing interior appearance. Built in 1881, the bridge spanned Poplar Creek north of Lancaster for over a hundred years. In the mid-1980s, badly deteriorated, with shotgun holes in its roof and other scars of vandalism, this outstanding structure appeared to be doomed. Fortunately, local residents made an effort to save, move, and restore it. It will sit for many years at its new home over Fetters Run at the back of the campus.

After checking out the bridge you'll next head north, briefly on the shoulder of State Route 37, then on country roads. Before long, you'll pass the James Walters property, where the old **McLeery Covered Bridge** lies. Built in 1864 as the bloody Civil War mercifully began to wind down, this bridge formerly spanned Walnut Creek. Facing destruction in 1983, it was rescued and moved by Walters, who has served as president of the Fairfield County Covered Bridge Association. Because one end rotted away, it is now substantially shorter than its original length of 110 feet.

You can get a good view from the road; if you wish to inspect it closer, request permission first.

Mellow roads take you next to tiny Lockville. In its park, sitting atop old canal locks, is the **Hartman Covered Bridge**. Built in 1888, it was moved here in 1967. It is also on the Fairfield-Canal Winchester route (see that route description for more about this bridge and the relationship between covered bridges and Ohio's canal system.)

From the sleepy park, flat roads lead to Pickerington's Sycamore Creek Park, where you'll find the **Zeller/Smith Covered Bridge** at the end of a park-spanning bike path. Originally constructed in 1891, the bridge presided over Sycamore Creek south of Pickerington until it was moved with funds from the Village Council in 1986. Here, it spans the same creek—a nice touch. A couple miles east of Pickerington is an optional, mile-long "out-and-back" ride to the private **Hizey Covered Bridge,** also built in 1891. It is nicely situated above Sycamore Creek on a private drive. If you care to get permission and examine it up close, you'll find an interesting interior. The design features a multiple queenpost—the only bridge in this book with arches. Moving on, you'll come to Millersport on the southwest shore of Buckeye Lake. There, on the Corn Festival Grounds, the **Holliday/Andrews Covered Bridge** sits behind an assortment of small carnival buildings. Built over Walnut Creek in 1897, this bridge undoubtedly looked more comfortable there than it does now, spanning a ditch-like ravine near buildings far more temporary. Incidentally, the annual Corn Festival takes place in late July/early August so, depending on whether or not you'd like to include it in this journey, plan accordingly.

A few moderate sized hills greet you as you approach this route's last relocated bridge outside of West Rushville. The **Baker/ Winegardner Covered Bridge** sits serenely over a small, secluded pond in a wooded area well behind Fairfield Union High School. This bridge was originally erected over nearby Little Rush Creek in 1871, the same year B.F. Goodrich began what would become his rubber manufacturing empire about a hundred miles north in Akron. The construction of a Rush Creek Conservancy dam would have doomed this noble little bridge had it not been moved here in 1981. From here, you have a fairly peaceful and undemanding ride back to the O.U-Lancaster campus. When returning from a long ride, the park-like setting near the John Bright #2 Bridge looks even more like the ideal resting spot than it did when you set off.

Directions to the Starting Point: The Lancaster-O.U. campus is on the east side of State Route 37 on the far northern edge of town. The John Bright #2 Covered Bridge is behind the campus's southernmost parking lot.

Pt.-Pt.	Cume	Turn	Street/Landmark
0.0	0.0	R	Exit O.U. parking lot onto **SR 37**. Busy road, so ride the (decent) shoulder.
0.5	0.5	L	**TR 250 (Rainbow Rd.)**
0.3	0.8	BR	**TR 273 (Stringtown Rd.)** at stop sign
0.5	1.3	S	Stop sign. Ride straight on **TR 273**
1.2	2.5	S	Cross Coonpath Rd. at stop sign
3.1	5.6	L	Onto **CR 17 (Pleasantville Rd.)** at stop sign (T)
0.7	6.3	S	Cross SR 158 at stop sign
0.3	6.6		On property on your left is the **McLeery Covered Bridge**
5.0	11.6	L	Briefly, onto **CR 36 (Carroll-Northern Rd.)** at stop sign. Iron bridge to your right
0.1	11.7	R	Back onto **CR 17**
0.6	12.3	S	*Cautiously* cross four-lane US 33 at stop sign, then *carefully* cross railroad tracks on the other side. Road becomes **TR 206**
0.9	13.2	R	Road veers sharply left next to old red brick Zion Lutheran Church; make a right turn immediately after the church.
0.2	13.4	L	**CR 20 (Pickerington Rd.)**
0.1	13.5	R	Into **Lockville Park**, with mulberry trees, picnic tables, old canal locks, and the **Hartman Covered Bridge**.

Pt.-Pt.	Cume	Turn	Street/Landmark
0.0	13.5	**L**	Back onto **CR 20**, after relaxing and checking out the bridge and canal locks
0.7	14.2	**S**	Cross bridge
0.7	14.9	**S**	Cross US 33 at traffic light
3.2	18.1	**R**	Turn at **Sycamore Creek Park** sign
0.3	18.4	**S**	Enter park. Just behind the parking lot is a rideable stone path; ride it past tennis courts, where it turns into a paved bike path.
0.4	18.8		**Zeller/Smith Covered Bridge** on your right. After visiting bridge, exit park at parking lot just beyond bridge
0.2	19.0	**R**	**CR 20 (Pickerington Rd.)**
0.1	19.1	**S**	Pass City Hall, on your right
0.1	19.2	**R**	At stop sign. Then turn **left** almost immediately onto **North Center St.,** at stop sign
1.7	20.9	**R**	**CR 7 (Refugee Rd.)** at stop sign
1.6	22.5		[*Optional: To view the private **Hizey Covered Bridge**, turn **left** on **TR 225 (Tollgate Rd.)**, ride 0.5 miles, and bridge is on left side of road. Then return to **CR 7** and resume route (**left** turn) at mile 22.5]
0.4	22.9	**L**	**TR 229 (Saylor Rd.)**
0.5	23.4	**S**	Cross bridge over Poplar Creek
1.3	24.7	**R**	**SR 204**
0.3	25.0	**S**	Continue straight where SR 204 bears south. Road becomes **TR 110 (Blacklick Rd.).** Flat farmland the next few miles.
4.1	29.1	**S**	Cross SR 158 at stop sign
0.6	29.7	**S**	Old brick church with cemetery on left side. Road becomes (rideable) gravel for the next half mile
0.5	30.2	**S**	Cross Cherry Lane. Old brick schoolhouse on your left. Pavement resumes
1.8	32.0	**L**	**SR 37**

Pt.-Pt.	Cume	Turn	Street/Landmark
0.5	32.5	**BR**	**SR 79**
0.6	33.1	**R**	**CR 58 (Millersport Rd.)**
1.7	34.8	**S**	Pass flashing lights
0.3	35.1	**S**	Enter **Millersport**. Road becomes **Lancaster Street**. Food and drink available
0.1	35.2	**S**	Traffic light. Continue straight
0.1	35.3	**L**	Onto **Chatauqua Blvd.**
0.4	35.7	**R**	Enter **Festival Grounds** at Gate 4 and ride/walk 0.2 mile* straight down stone path past fair buildings, behind which sits the **Holliday/Andrews Covered Bridge**. After visiting bridge, return same way to Gate 4. (*This not on Cume mileage)
0.0	35.7	**L**	Backtrack on **Chataqua Blvd.**
0.4	36.1	**L**	Onto **Lancaster St./SR 204** at (T) stop sign
0.6	36.7	**S**	Continue straight where SR 204 bears left. Road becomes **CR 58 (Millersport Rd.)**
0.5	37.2	**L**	**TR 392 (Geiger Rd.)**
1.5	38.7	**S**	Cross CR 62 at stop sign
1.3	40.0	**R**	**TR 419 (Cattail Rd.)**
1.0	41.0	**S**	Cross CR 11 at stop sign
1.1	42.1	**S**	Cross SR 188 at stop sign
0.4	42.5	**S**	Cross SR 256 at stop sign
2.1	44.6	**L**	**CR 17 (Pleasantville Rd.)**
0.4	45.0	**S**	Cross bridge
2.2	47.2	**BR**	At fork, remain on **CR 17**
1.0	48.2	**R**	Onto **SR 664**. Some rolling hills into Rushville
2.6	50.8	**S**	Enter **Rushville**. Supplies available
0.1	50.9	**S**	Traffic light
0.4	51.3	**R**	**US 22**. Ride with caution, on shoulder
1.5	52.8	**S**	Cross bridge
0.8	53.6	**L**	Onto grounds of **Fairfield Union High School**. Ride stone path behind parking lot, and pass football field

Pt.-Pt.	Cume	Turn	Street/Landmark
0.4	54.0	**R**	Down grass path
0.1	54.1		The **Baker/Winegardner Covered Bridge**. After visiting the bridge and perhaps relaxing by the peaceful pond, back track to leave the school grounds
0.5	54.6	**L**	**US 22**, (then near-immediate **right**)
0.0	54.6	**R**	**Fairfield Union Rd.**, right after turning onto **US 22**
1.0	55.6	**L**	**CR 31 (Coonpath Rd.)** at stop sign
1.2	56.8	**S**	Cross bridge
1.0	57.8	**S**	Cross CR 60 at four-way stop sign
2.2	60.0	**S**	Cross SR 188 at stop sign
0.8	60.8	**L**	Onto **TR 393 (Old Millersport Rd.)** Ride through residential neighborhood
1.1	61.9	**R**	Onto **TR 250 (Rainbow Dr.)** at (T) stop sign
0.2	62.1	**S**	Stop sign
0.5	62.6	**L**	Turn left at "T" intersection
0.3	62.9	**L**	**SR 37**. Ride on the shoulder
0.5	63.4	**L**	Into **O.U.-Lancaster** parking lot. End of ride

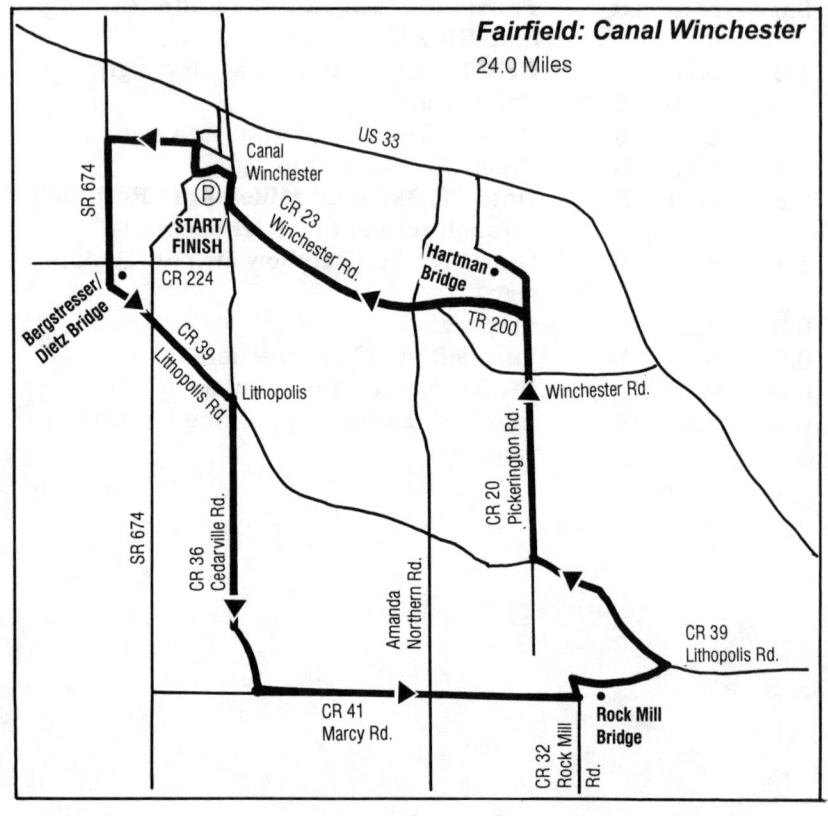

Fairfield: Canal Winchester
24.0 Miles

US 33

SR 674

Canal
Winchester

CR 23
Winchester Rd.

**START/
FINISH**

CR 224

**Hartman
Bridge**

TR 200

Bergstresser/
Dietz Bridge

CR 39
Lithopolis Rd.

Lithopolis

Winchester Rd.

SR 674

CR 36
Cedarville Rd.

Amanda
Northern Rd.

CR 20
Pickerington Rd.

CR 39
Lithopolis Rd.

CR 41
Marcy Rd.

CR 32
Rock Mill
Rd.

**Rock Mill
Bridge**

Fairfield: Canal Winchester—24.0 miles

Terrain: Flat to rolling, with several mildly demanding hills.

Road Conditions: All paved and mostly smooth.

Traffic: Light to moderate throughout, but can get moderately heavy on County Route 23 near the end of the ride.

Points of Interest: Bergstresser/Dietz Covered Bridge; Rock Mill Covered Bridge; Hartman Covered Bridge; old canal locks.

This compact ride begins in the rural southeast corner of largely urban Franklin County, touching this county's last standing covered bridge before going on to visit two other covered bridges in Fairfield County. Taking its name from the beautifully-flowered fields that settlers found here in the early 1800s, today Fairfield County is semi-rural, with numerous small towns and one fairly large city: Lancaster, its seat of county government. This one county has built—and dismantled, abandoned, moved, or simply given away—more covered bridges than any other county in Ohio. Fairfield County has constructed over 270 covered bridges over the years, a number that has steadily dwindled to fewer than 50 by 1950, less than 30 by 1970, and has dropped even further to 15 today, five of which sit on privately-owned property. Some years ago, the Southern Ohio Covered Bridge Association provided a tour-map of Fairfield County covered bridges that included a single 22-mile route that featured an amazing 20 bridges! Such a tour is no longer even remotely possible here—or anywhere else in Ohio for that matter. However, on this tour you will visit two of the county's remaining covered bridges, including its last "active" one, and on the other two Fairfield County rides you can visit most of the county's other publicly-accessible bridges. Most of Fairfield County's remaining covered bridges will likely be protected and maintained for the foreseeable future.

The ride starts in pleasant little Canal Winchester, in a public parking lot near the Shade Restaurant (a good spot to satisfy your post-ride appetite). From Canal Winchester, pedal south on mellow State Route 674, soon reaching the fabulously-maintained **Dietz** or **Bergstressor Covered Bridge**. This 125-foot long bridge has the dubious distinction of being the last remaining covered bridge original to Franklin County, which at one time boasted over a hundred of these unique structures. In 1887, county officials responded to demands from local residents for a new bridge over Walnut Creek by choosing between bids for a covered structure and an iron bridge. At $2,690, the bid for the covered version was about $1,000 cheaper than the iron bridge, and fortunately economics drove the selection process. Always well maintained, the bridge received a thorough renovation in 1991 that included new siding and a new roof. Now closed to vehicular traffic (you can walk or ride over it, though), this bridge could easily last several more centuries for other generations to enjoy—it even co-exists peacefully with a new housing subdivision that has sprung up across the street.

On your way to the next covered bridge, you'll pass through the sleepy little village of Lithopolis. If you decide to grab a meal or stop to rest, I suggest the tranquil Wagnall's Memorial, a library and community center on East Columbus Street. This Tudor-Gothic structure, made of native freestone, was the estate of the Wagnall's family, publishers of the Funk & Wagnall's Encyclopedia, among other books. In addition to original Norman Rockwell paintings, a small garden on the side and rear provide a perfect place to take a quiet break. Please respect the signs stating that bikes should be kept off the brick sidewalks.

After leaving Lithopolis, you'll ride rolling county roads on your way to the renowned **Rock Mill Covered Bridge**. The only covered bridge in the county that still carries motor vehicle traffic, at 37 feet long it is also the fourth shortest in Ohio. Artists, photographers, and plain admirers of beauty often visit Rock Mill Bridge. It is set atop a blackhand sandstone gorge with sheer walls that rise above the rushing Hocking River. The vista below features gorgeous waterfalls. Looking down from the bridge or nearby rock ledges—great spots to view or photograph the bridge—you'll see deep pools in the stream created by swirling sand-filled melt-waters left behind by retreating glaciers thousands of years ago. Allow yourself time to soak in the splendor of this old bridge and its exquisite natural setting. A nearby stone quarry provided rock for the bridge abutment of the Rock Mill and other covered bridges in the area. Nearby, on private farm property, sits Rock Mill, built in 1824, but serving as a barn since around the turn of the century. The bridge was built in 1901—two years before Ohio native Orville Wright made his famous powered aircraft flight at Kitty Hawk—for a total cost of $575. The work was done by prolific local builder Jacob R. Brandt, nicknamed "Blue Jeans" because of his favorite attire. It is no surprise that he preferred this durable cotton fabric because, after all, with the help of steel I-beam reinforcements that have been added, his quaint and useful structure has proven most resilient and likely will stand for many years to come.

You'll encounter some modest hills and splendid vistas riding to this route's final stop, the **Hartman Covered Bridge**. This short (48-foot) bridge was originally built in 1888 and moved from here to the Lockville Village Park in 1967. It now sits over old locks from the Ohio and Erie Canal. This is a pleasantly fitting setting for a transplanted Ohio covered bridge, because the state's massive canal building projects in the early and mid-19th century led to the construction of many covered bridges to cross this network of meandering canals. In a unique design twist, some of the canal-crossing covered bridges had trapdoors installed in their floors so that farmers could shovel grain directly into canal boats waiting below. The bridges and canals worked fine until the newly-formed railroad companies began laying track throughout Ohio and the rest of the nation in the 1830s, dooming the once prosperous Ohio canal system to a footnote in history. By the turn of the century, the canal system that once connected Lake Erie to the Ohio River declined, and most of its bridges saw little traffic.

After checking out the bridge and old canal locks, perhaps enjoying a shady break in the park's picnic area, or maybe even eating a few berries off of the big old mulberry tree near the road, you'll have about a five-mile ride back to Canal Winchester. A note of caution: Be careful on County Route 23 because, although it travels through pretty countryside, it can get quite busy.

Directions to the Starting Point: Canal Winchester is just south-east of Columbus, Ohio, and is easily accessible from either direction via US 33. When heading east from Columbus, pass the Canal Winchester exit and get off the freeway at the High Street exit. If coming by way of Lancaster, turn left onto High Street from US 33. After exiting the freeway, the public parking lot is located downtown off of High Street. Look for the "Free Parking" sign on the east side of the street next to the Shade Restaurant. The parking spots are just down the alley, behind the post office.

Pt.-Pt.	Cume	Turn	Street/Landmark
0.0	0.0	L	Exit parking lot/alley on **S. High St.**
0.1	0.1	R	**Columbus St.**
0.1	0.2	L	**Washington St**. At traffic light. This street soon turns into **SR 674**
0.2	0.4	BR	With **SR 674**
0.1	0.5	BL	With **SR 674**
0.4	0.9	S	Cross over bridge.
0.3	1.2	R	**CR 224.** Immediately encounter the **Bergstresser/Dietz Bridge**. Use caution if you ride over; there are gaps between the floor planks. After visiting bridge, go back to **SR 674.**
0.0	1.2	R	Continue south on **SR 674**
1.1	2.3	L	Onto **CR 39 (Lithopolis Rd.)** at traffic light.
0.5	2.8	S	Pass "Entering Lithopolis" sign. Food and refreshments available here
0.7	3.5	S	Pass under traffic light.
0.2	3.7	R	**CR 36 (Cedar Hill Rd.)** at traffic light. This road rolls some.
0.1	3.8	S	Pass cemetery on your right.
2.0	5.8	S	Cross one-lane bridge.

Pt.-Pt.	Cume	Turn	Street/Landmark
1.5	7.3	**L**	Onto **CR 41 (Marcy Rd.)** at stop sign (T)
2.1	9.4	**S**	Stop sign. Cross Amanda Northern Rd. **CR 41** continues slightly to right after intersection.
1.7	11.1	**L**	Onto **CR 32 (Rock Mill Rd.)** at stop sign.
0.1	11.2	**SR**	**CR 32** turns sharply right.
1.1	12.3		**Rock Mill Covered Bridge**. Hang around a little to soak in the scenery.
0.1	12.4	**BL**	**CR 39 (Lithopolis Rd.)** at stop sign.
2.2	14.6	**S**	Cross bridge.
0.8	15.4	**R**	**CR 20 (Pickerington Rd.)** at curve signs. Immediately a small uphill.
0.5	15.9	**S**	Climb first of several hills.
1.8	17.7	**S**	Stop sign. Cross Winchester Rd.
0.7	18.4	**S**	Cross bridge.
0.4	18.8	**L**	Into **Lockville Park**. Straight ahead to picnic area, old canal locks, and **Hartman Covered Bridge**.
0.0	18.8	**R**	**CR 20**. Backtrack briefly.
0.5	19.3	**R**	**TR 200 (Jefferson Rd.)**
0.2	19.5	**S**	Cross bridge.
1.0	20.5	**BR**	After stop sign, road becomes **CR 23 (Winchester Rd.)** *Caution:* this rolling road can get busy with vehicle traffic
2.8	23.3	**BR**	Bear right and cross bridge
0.3	23.6	**BL**	Re-enter **Canal Winchester**
0.3	23.9	**L**	Onto **S. High St.** at stop sign
0.1	24.0	**L**	Left into parking lot. End of ride.

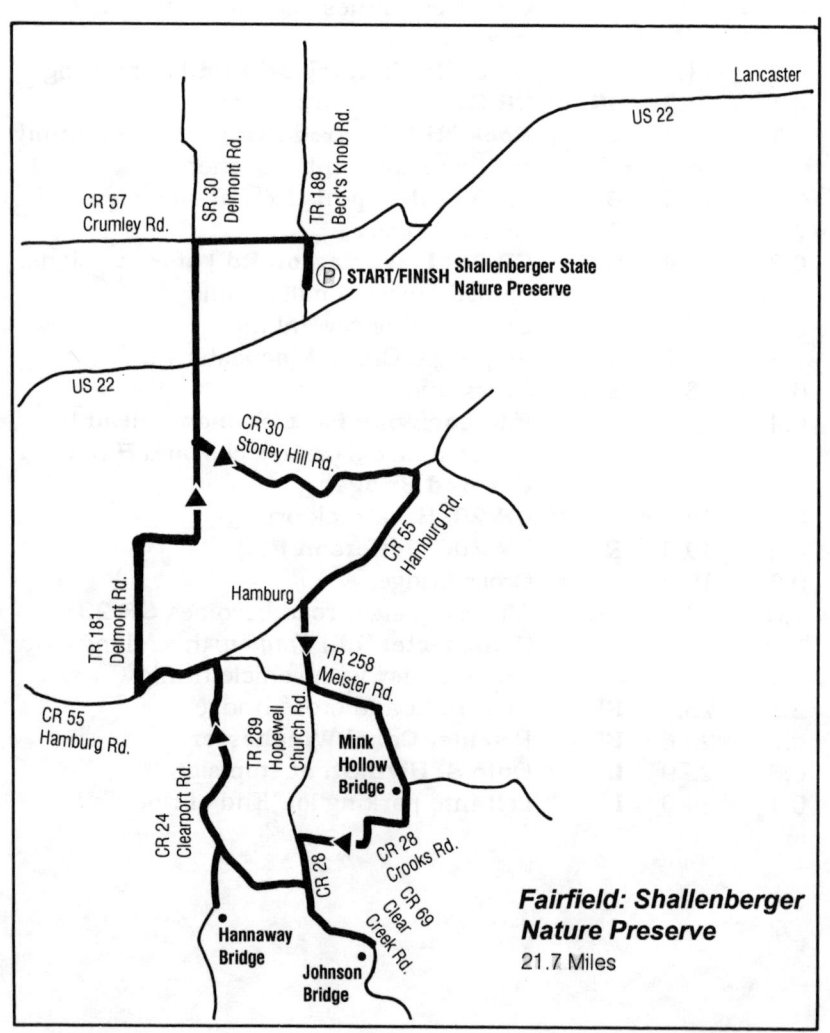

Fairfield: Shallenberger Nature Preserve—21.7 miles

Terrain: Mostly pleasantly rolling, with a few sizable hills.

Road Conditions: All paved and generally excellent, with one short stretch of rough road surface.

Traffic: Very little.

Points of Interest: Shallenberger State Nature Preserve; Mink Hollow Covered Bridge; Johnson Covered Bridge; Hannaway Covered Bridge; Beautiful scenery throughout—tree-leaf canopies, Amish country, and splendid vistas of rolling countryside.

This route is one of the shortest and one of the sweetest of any in this *RIDE GUIDE*. It starts and ends at one neat place, it is entirely rural, it traverses good roads through extraordinary countryside, and its three covered bridges do not disappoint.

Those bridges are all bypassed by the road that they formerly supported. If you did or will do the **Fairfield Moving On Route**, where all the bridges have been moved, this route's bridges make a good point of comparison. Moving and bypassing are the two main methods of preserving a bridge that no longer carries regular traffic. All things considered, I prefer bypassing because it leaves the old structures in their original settings. Then again, the moved bridges are generally safer from vandals; you'll see more graffiti on bypassed bridges, and they are definitely more susceptible to the occasional arsonist.

This ride begins from the small parking lot of the Shallenberger State Nature Preserve. The centerpiece of the preserve is Allen Knob, which towers high above the surrounding area as you approach. Allen Knob, and the smaller Ruby Knob nearby, are both comprised of highly resilient sandstone deposited by an ancient inland sea, and have weathered the natural ravages of time and the Ice Age glaciers that dumped rocky debris at their base before retreating. While the base of the knobs supports an abundance of fern, flower, shrub, and tree species, chestnut oak and mountain laurel dominate on the knobs. After your ride, you should have enough energy to enjoy a hike down the well-marked trails that begin just behind the parking lot. Follow the Arrowhead Trail to the overlook trail, which winds up the knob. Up on top you receive a spectacular view of the rolling countryside that you just pedaled through. (In the spring and autumn, there is far less leafy obstruction of the view!)

But first, you'll want to see the countryside—and three charming bridges in its midst—from the seat of your bike. Leaving the preserve, you'll immediately encounter a couple of modest hills, then rolling roads through tranquil wooded farmlands. The first few miles, knobs dot the landscape. You'll soon reach the little **Mink Hollow Covered Bridge**. Built in 1887, the Mink Hollow Bridge has a multiple kingpost truss with an unusual double kingpost center panel. It was recently bypassed, but you can still (cautiously) ride through it. It sits placidly over the clear running waters of Arney Mill Run and is surrounded by a park area with a picnic table. Relax for a spell.

After taking a break, it's a pleasant few miles to the **Johnson Covered Bridge**. Like all of this route's bridges, it has two full-length windows protected by awnings. It was built in 1887, the same year as the Mink Hollow Bridge, but spans Clear Creek. It sits on stone abutments strengthened by poured concrete. Recently bypassed, it was treated to renovations in 1996, including new wood-shake shingles like those that were once utilized on most covered bridges. Most covered bridge roofs have since been replaced with tin roofs.

A few peaceful miles get you to this route's third bridge, the somewhat more weathered **Hannaway Covered Bridge**. Built in 1901, the same year Ohio native President William McKinley was assassinated, this bridge keeps surviving above the banks of Clear Creek. It was scheduled to be either moved or demolished in 1987, but thankfully the demolition never went forward. It's beginning to lean a bit now, and is missing some roofing and a few siding planks, but overall appears capable of hanging on until it can be properly saved.

Your return trip includes rolling Amish farmlands and majestic vistas from one of the county's high points—yes, there is a steep hill here, too. However, you should have plenty of energy left at trip's end to take a stroll through the nature preserve.

Directions to the Starting Point: The parking lot to Shallenberger State Nature Preserve is on the east side of Beck's Knob Road, a quarter mile north off of US 22, several miles west/southwest of Lancaster.

Pt.-Pt.	Cume	Turn	Street/Landmark
0.0	0.0	R	Exit parking lot onto **TR 189 (Beck's Knob Road)**
0.5	0.5	L	**CR 57 (Crumley Rd.)** at stop sign.
0.4	0.9	S	Old church on the hill to your right
0.6	1.5	L	**SR 30 (Delmont Rd.)**
0.6	2.1	S	Climb first good hill of ride.
0.4	2.5	S	Cautiously cross US 22 at stop sign.
0.6	3.1	BL	At fork in road. Still **CR 30** (but now **Stoney Hill Rd**.)
2.3	5.4	R	Onto **CR 55 (Hamburg Rd.)** at stop sign.
1.0	6.4	S	Cross bridge.
0.4	6.8	L	**TR 289 (Hopewell Church Rd.)** at **Hamburg**, a tiny gathering of houses. There's a playground at the turn.
0.8	7.6	L	**TR 258 (Meister Rd.)** at stop sign *Caution* approaching it during a fairly steep descent.
0.7	8.3	R	**CR 28 (Crooks Rd.)**. Interesting log house on right at turn, with a children's covered footbridge.
0.1	8.4	L	At **Mink Hollow Covered Bridge**. Picnic area just before bridge. You can ride through bridge, but do it cautiously. After visiting the bridge, return to road via the short stone road on the other side of bridge.

Pt.-Pt.	Cume	Turn	Street/Landmark
0.0	8.4	**L**	**CR 28**, at stop sign south of bridge.
0.5	8.9	**BR**	At fork right after bridge.
0.5	9.4	**S**	Cross bridge.
1.1	10.5	**L**	**CR 28** (now **Hopewell Church Rd**.), at stop sign.
0.4	10.9	**L**	**CR 69 (Clear Creek Rd.)** at stop sign.
0.1	11.0	**S**	Hopewell Church and cemetery on left
0.4	11.4	**S**	**Johnson Covered Bridge** on right.
0.1	11.5	**R**	Onto short access road (not on cume miles) to bridge. After visiting, return to road's stop sign.
0.0	11.5	**L**	At stop sign. Backtrack on **CR 69.**
1.1	12.6	**BR**	As you cross bridge, bear right.
0.4	13.0	**L**	**CR 24 (Clearport Rd.)** at stop sign.
0.1	13.1	**S**	Mt. Carmel Church on your right.
0.1	13.2	**L**	With the **Hannaway Covered Bridge** in sight about 100 yards ahead, look for narrow walking path on your left—it is your access to the bridge. After visiting bridge, backtrack on **CR 24** (Ride north, beyond last turn)
1.0	14.2	**S**	Cross bridge
1.0	15.2	**L**	**CR 55 (Hamburg Rd.)** at T. You are entering well-kept Amish country.
0.4	15.6	**S**	Cross bridge in valley.
0.3	15.9	**R**	**TR 181 (Delmont Rd.)**
0.5	16.4	**S**	Cross bridge over Muddy Prairie Run
0.8	17.2		Roads bears sharply right
0.1	17.3	**S**	Moderately steep climb
0.4	17.7		Road bears sharply left
0.9	18.6	**S**	Stop sign. Continue straight. You are approaching one of the county's high points—great vistas ahead.
0.6	19.2	**S**	Stop sign. Cautiously cross US 22.
1.0	20.2	**R**	**Onto CR 57 (Crumley Rd.)** at stop sign. Knob country again
0.3	20.5	**S**	Cross bridge

Pt.-Pt.	Cume	Turn	Street/Landmark
0.7	21.2	**R**	**TR 189 (Beck's Knob Rd.)**
0.5	21.7	**L**	Into nature preserve parking lot. End of route.

The Rock Mill Covered Bridge was built in 1901 for a total cost of $575. At 37 feet long, it is the fourth-shortest covered bridge in Ohio, and the only one in Fairfield County that still carries motor vehicle traffic.

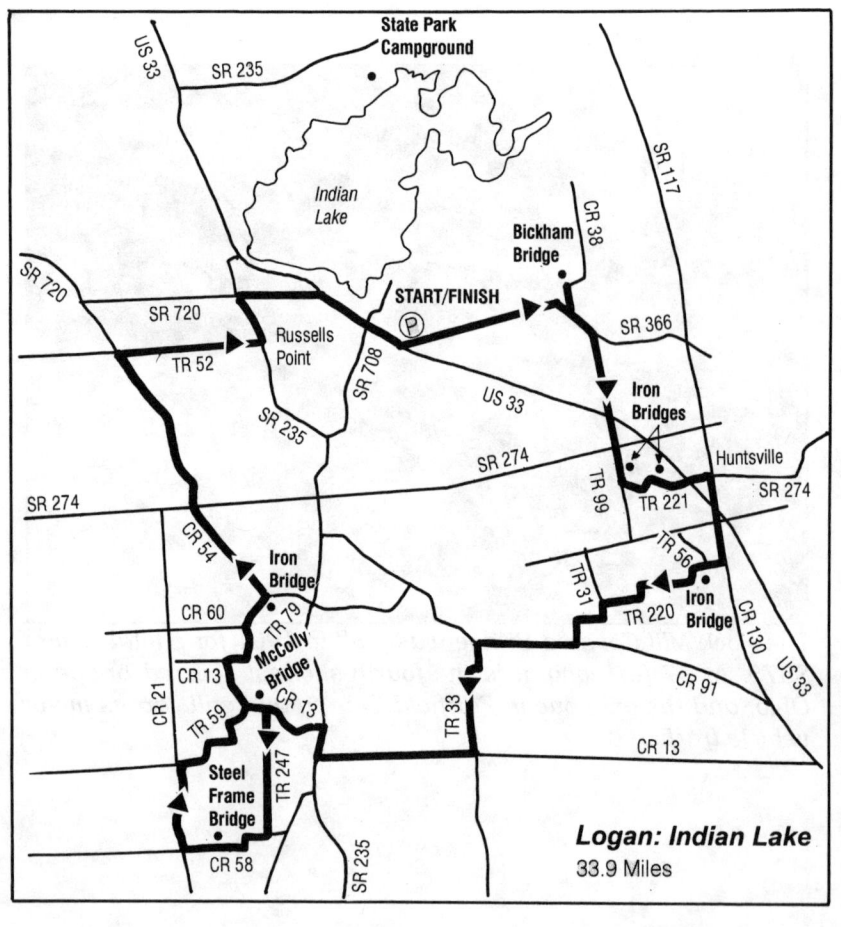

Logan: Indian Lake
33.9 Miles

Logan: Indian Lake—33.9 miles

Terrain: Flat to rolling, with several moderate hills.

Road Conditions: All paved, generally smooth roads.

Traffic: Moderate on State Route 366 at the beginning and end of the ride, moderate to heavy levels of traffic on weekends and during vacation season, light to nonexistent on the county and township backroads.

Points of Interest: Indian Lake, Bickham Covered Bridge, McColly Covered Bridge, old iron bridges, Amish country.

Logan County takes its name from General Benjamin Logan and boasts of having the highest point between the Rocky Mountains and the Appalachians, but don't worry—this high ground is not on this route. About a dozen covered bridges once dotted the county and the area was once home to four American Indian tribes—the Wyandots, Cherokees, Roundheads, and Delawares. Some of the long-gone covered bridges reflected a Native American feel, with names like Muchinippi and Buckongelas. Two covered bridges still remain in the region, including the **Bickham Bridge** and the **McColly Bridge**, both of which are Howe truss bridges built in the 1870s. On this ride you will visit both.

The ride begins at a parking lot just across the road from the southern shore of **Indian Lake**. The second largest man-made lake in Ohio, Indian Lake was formed in the 1850s by building a dam at the source of the Great Miami River. A series of small kettle lakes were covered by the expanded lake. Indian Lake was then used as a feeder lake to keep the nearby Miami and Erie Canal at a constant depth of four feet. After Ohio's canal system failed with the advent of steam-powered trains, the state took over control of the lake and, in the early 1900s, turned it into a recreational area. Once known as "The Midwest's Million Dollar Playground" in the years leading up to World War II, amusement parks and dance halls attracted hordes of tourists and big-band performers like Glenn Miller and Guy Lombardo.

Today, the million-dollar mystique has faded, but the lake is still a popular recreational draw with 29 miles of shoreline, 69 (mostly tiny) islands, and tons of fish. Exiting the parking lot's east outlet, you'll ride along the lake's southern spillway that feeds the Great Miami River. You'll cross the river at mile 0.2 where a covered bridge once spanned the waterway. Exercise care when riding on State Route 366; although traffic is generally not fast, it can be busy, especially on weekends during the vacation season. (If possible, this would make a good weekday route.)

Getting off State Route 366 onto County Route 38, you'll soon arrive at the **Bickham Covered Bridge**. It was built over the south fork of the Little Miami River in 1877. In its early years, the bridge supported a lot of foot- and hoof-powered traffic before engine-powered vehicles ever crossed over it. This bridge is still up to the task today as it carries more daily traffic than most remaining covered bridges, yet remains in good repair.

Heading south, you'll encounter two old iron bridges, then the tiny town of Huntsville, home of two dairy stands (both of which offer refreshing milkshakes). Continuing on, the roads begin to roll and weave more; they also become much quieter. Along the way, you may encounter Amish families in horse-drawn buggies as you approach the **McColly Covered Bridge**. While conducting research for this ride, the McColly Covered Bridge was listed as "active," but when I arrived on the scene it had been closed to vehicle traffic with guardrails installed at both ends. I have since learned that the county plans to move it about 50 feet downstream to new foundations, where it will one day be completely overhauled. Built in 1876, this bridge is in a lovely setting over the Great Miami River and is well worth the visit. Some years ago, repairs on the bridge included the patching of a hole on the bridge deck where a wiener roast had apparently gotten out of hand. Don't have a barbecue; just enjoy a snack and some R&R at this quaint old bridge.

Leaving the McColly Bridge, you'll ride on serene, rolling roads through Amish country. The route crosses several other old iron bridges, including a splendid frame bridge built in 1894 by the Iron Substitute Bridge Company of Columbus. The name of this firm is representative of what was going on at the time—the promotion of iron bridges as "substitutes" for wooden bridges. Although we can lament the resulting decrease in covered bridges, iron bridges like this one still have vastly more character than the nondescript concrete bridges being built today to replace them—at a much higher price, and with a much shorter lifespan. Before returning to the starting point, you'll ride near the other end of the **McColly Bridge**, cross several more old iron bridges, and pass a country cemetery and a large former Indian reservation. Until you get close to Indian Lake again, the roads will be peaceful, and any vehicles you do encounter are likely to be horse-drawn.

If you'd like to take a refreshing post-ride swim, the public beach is located on the western shore of the lake; shoreline bikeways that reach most of the way there begin just northwest of Russell's Point. If you care to camp while in the area, private campgrounds surround the lake and the state park campground is off of State Route 235, on the lake's northern shore, where there is also a small public beach.

Directions to the Starting Point: The parking lot is off State Route 366 opposite Indian Lake, just east of the Russell's Point business district. It has restrooms, a picnic table or two, and plenty of parking.

Pt.-Pt.	Cume	Turn	Street/Landmark
0.0	0.0	**R**	Exit parking lot's east outlet onto **SR 366**. Ride carefully.
0.2	0.2	**S**	Cross Great Miami River head. Shoulder improves for awhile—ride it.
1.8	2.0	**BL**	**CR 38**. Check for traffic front and back before turning.
0.2	2.2	**L**	Still **CR 38**. Left at stop sign.

Pt.-Pt.	Cume	Turn	Street/Landmark
0.2	2.4	S	The **Bickham Covered Bridge**. After visiting bridge, backtrack on **CR 38**.
0.2	2.6	BL	Left at fork in road.
0.1	2.7	L	**SR 366**, at stop sign. Continue cautious riding.
0.4	3.1	R	**TR 99**.
1.1	4.2	S	Stop sign. Cross US 33.
1.5	5.7	S	Stop sign. Cross SR 274.
0.4	6.1	S	Cross old **iron bridge**.
0.1	6.2	L	**TR 221**. Narrow, very low traffic. Road meanders.
0.2	6.4	S	**Old iron bridge** over Cherokee Creek.
0.9	7.3	S	Stop sign. Cross US 33 again.
0.3	7.6	R	**Rude Street** in Huntsville.
0.2	7.8	R	**Lima Street** (no sign). Food, including cold, thick milkshakes, available in both directions. This road becomes **CR 130** after overpass.
1.4	9.2	R	**TR 56**. "Piano Lessons" sign at the turn.
0.2	9.4	S	**Old iron bridge**, built in 1910
0.1	9.5	S	**TR 220** (TR 56 turns right)
1.8	11.3	L	**TR 31** (T) at stop sign. No street sign, concrete post on left.
0.6	11.9	R	**CR 91**.
1.4	13.3	L	**TR 33**. Turn left just as CR 91 curves to the right.
1.4	14.7	R	**CR 13**. At stop sign.
2.1	16.8	R	**SR 235** (T). At stop sign.
0.2	17.0	L	**CR 13** (right after crossing bridge). You are now in Amish territory.
1.0	18.0	S	The **McColly Covered Bridge**. After visiting bridge, backtrack on **CR 13**.
0.3	18.3	R	**TR 247**. You will encounter some moderate-sized hills the next few miles.
1.5	19.8	R	**CR 58** (T) at stop sign. There is no street sign, but you'll see a "One lane bridge" sign to your right.

Pt.-Pt.	Cume	Turn	Street/Landmark
0.2	20.0	**S**	**Old steel frame bridge**, built 1894 by the Iron Substitute Bridge Co. in peaceful setting over the Great Miami River.
0.4	20.4	**S**	**Old iron bridge**.
0.6	21.0	**R**	**CR 21** at stop sign.
1.1	22.1	**R**	**TR 59.**
1.4	23.5	**L**	**CR 13** at stop sign. 0.1 mile to your right is the other end of the **McColly Bridge.**
0.4	23.9	**S**	Country cemetery on your left.
0.2	24.1	**R**	**TR 79**. CR 13 turns left.
0.8	24.9	**R**	**CR 60** at stop sign. On your right is **iron bridge** that you'll cross immediately after turning.
0.5	25.4	**L**	**CR 54**.
1.6	27.0	**S**	Stop sign. Cross SR 274.
1.0	28.0	**S**	Sign posted on right about this area's past as a large Indian reservation.
1.4	29.4	**R**	**TR 52**.
2.0	31.4	**L**	**SR 235** at stop sign. Ride the shoulder.
0.6	32.0	**R**	**SR 720** right after "Lakeview" sign.
0.8	32.8	**BR**	Remain on **SR 720**.
0.5	33.3	**S**	Traffic light. Cross US 33.
0.0	33.3	**R**	**SR 366** at traffic light, almost immediately after previous one. Enter Russell's Point. Post-ride food and refreshments available.
0.2	33.5	**S**	Stop sign.
0.4	33.9	**R**	Into parking lot. End of ride.

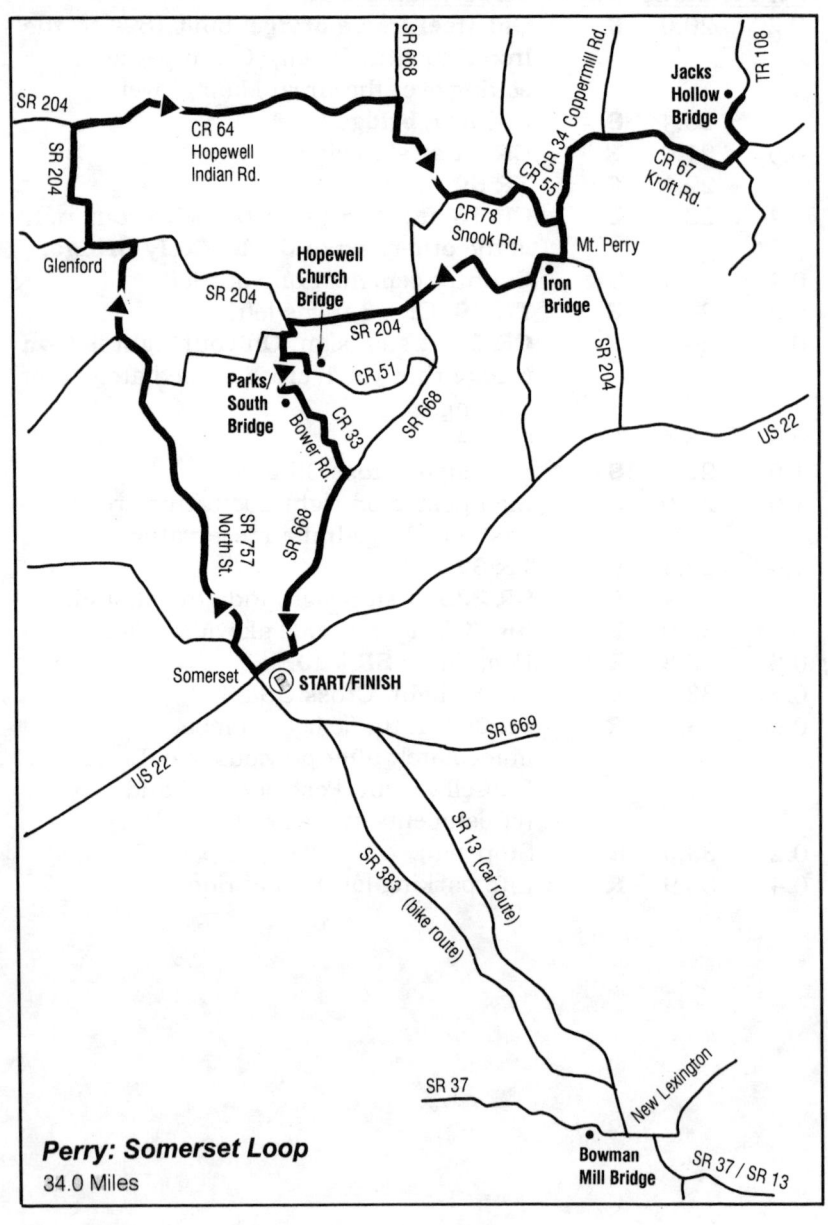

SR 204

SR 668

CR CR 34 Coppermill Rd.

TR 108

Jacks
Hollow •
Bridge

SR 204

CR 64
Hopewell
Indian Rd.

CR 55

CR 67
Kroft Rd.

CR 78
Snook Rd.

Mt. Perry

Glenford

Hopewell
Church
Bridge

SR 204

Iron
Bridge

SR 204

SR 204

SR 204

CR 51

US 22

Parks/
South
Bridge

CR 33

SR 668

Bower Rd.

SR 757
North St.

SR 668

Somerset

Ⓟ START/FINISH

SR 669

US 22

SR 13 (car route)

SR 383 (bike route)

New Lexington

SR 37

Perry: Somerset Loop

34.0 Miles

SR 37 / SR 13

Bowman
Mill Bridge

Perry: Somerset Loop—34.0 miles

Terrain: Somewhat hilly the first and last few miles. Otherwise, moderately rolling with patches of flatland and one or two strenuous hills.

Road Conditions: Paved and generally smooth, except for 2.8 miles of gravel roads near the first covered bridge.

Traffic: Generally light. Moderate traffic on State Route 204.

Points of Interest: Historic Somerset; Jacks Hollow Covered Bridge; Hopewell Church Covered Bridge; Parks/South Covered Bridge.

Named for Commodore Oliver Hazard Perry, "The Hero of Lake Erie" in the War of 1812, Perry County is primarily rural. The northeastern part of the county—where most of this ride is centered—is rich in history. Several dozen earthen Indian mounds and enclosures have been found in this region. Also discovered: mastodon teeth weighing as much as 17 pounds apiece. Closer to the present, Perry County once was Ohio's leading producer of coal. In 1884 a labor dispute flared—literally—in the southern part of the county, where mine workers set a coal car afire and pushed it into a mine where it started other fires that burned for decades.

As long as those fires lasted, the three covered bridges featured in this route have been carrying traffic for a much longer period of time. One of the bridges even survived a fire to stand today. Perry County once had dozens of covered bridges. Today, only these three, another transplanted from Fairfield County that now sits on private property, and Bowman Mill Covered Bridge at the County Fairgrounds in New Lexington, still survive.

This loop begins in quaint, historic Somerset and departs for points north. After parking on a nearby side street, begin at the town's central "Pigfoot Square." You can't miss the towering statue of Civil War General Phil Sheridan. Sheridan, who spent much of his childhood in Somerset, made a famous, perilous ride from Winchester to Cedar Creek during the Civil War, securing victory for the Union. This earned him national admiration (at least in the north!) and a resting place in Arlington National Cemetery. He had a home built here for his parents, and it still stands on State Route 13. His boyhood home is just west off State Route 13 on Sheridan Avenue.

Your own ride will not earn you similar fame. Nor should it be perilous. But it will earn you a resting place back in old Somerset when you finish. Leaving town on State Route 757, you'll encounter some roller-coaster hills and very picturesque country. After touching little Glenford—refreshments are available at the small general store—you'll head for some quiet country roads, including a mile of rideable gravel on Snook Road. These roads lead to shaded, gravel TR 108, which takes you to **Jacks Hollow Covered Bridge**, 0.9 miles away. The gravel on TR 108 makes for difficult riding, unless you're on a mountain bike. Even if you are on a mountain bike, we strongly suggest walking your bike, at least up and down the hills on this rough road. Local builder William Dean, who also built the Parks/South Bridge on this loop and over twenty other Perry County covered bridges that are no longer in existence, built Jacks Hollow Bridge in 1879.

Just north of the bridge there once stood a pottery and a sawmill powered by the waters of Kents Run. The pottery and sawmill are long gone, but the bridge lives on and Kents Run continues to flow beneath it. The creek banks east of the bridge are accessible and suitable spots for a view or photograph. The bridge's sturdy old multiple kingpost trusses were damaged by arson a few years ago, causing the bridge to be closed for repair work. It is missing some siding now, and graffiti adorns its walls, but on this backroad, the Jacks Hollow Bridge should last many more years.

Leaving, you'll probably want to walk your bike up the immediate steep gravel road. Then, you'll backtrack on pretty County Routes 67 and 34, cross over an excellent old iron bridge, and enter tiny Mt. Perry. DJ's Market, open seven days a week, sells groceries, cold drinks, sandwiches, subs and pizzas. Then, it's onward through a region famous for silica deposits prized by glass makers before finally encountering **Hopewell Church Covered Bridge**. This 55-foot bridge was built in 1874 over Painter Run for just $4.85 per linear foot. It was named for Hopewell Church, which you will pass as you turn onto the bridge's road. The church's first congregation gathered a good half-century before the old bridge was even built.

Just down County Route 33 is **Parks** or **South Covered Bridge**. Built in 1883 by William Dean (who also built Jacks Hollow Bridge), this structure is considered "an outstanding example of the multiple kingpost truss," by bridge historian Miriam Wood. Like the Hopewell Church Bridge, this structure also spans Painter Run; when you cross Painter Run, ride slowly and carefully, as the floor is not very cycle-friendly.

After visiting the bridge and perhaps picking some roadside honeysuckle, you face just four miles of fairly hilly riding back to Somerset. As you reach town, a Dairy Freeze beckons.

Directions to Starting Point: Somerset, in northern Perry County, east/southeast of Columbus, is accessible via US 22 and State Routes 13, 757, 668, and 669. These all merge on the town square, watched over by General Sheridan. Park your car on any nearby side street.

Directions to the Fairgrounds: To see the **Bowman Mill Bridge,** take a side trip to the County Fairgrounds in New Lexington, where the bridge has stood since 1987. Follow State Route 13 south out of Somerset to New Lexington and turn west on State Route 37 for 0.3 miles. If you go by bicycle, turn south on State Route 383 off of State Route 13 a couple miles out of town; State Route 13 will turn into County Route 60, Old Somerset Road, at the old St. Joseph's Church—the first Catholic parish in Ohio. This road rejoins State Route 13 just north of New Lexington; pick up the driving directions from this point.

Pt.-Pt.	Cume	Turn	Street/Landmark
0.0	0.0		Ride north from the town square on **Columbus St. (SR 13).** You're on the right track if you see the post office on your right as you leave the square
0.4	0.4	R	**North St. (SR 757)**
0.3	0.7	S	*Caution* on steep, curving downhill
4.4	5.1	S	Old church on right, cemetery on left
0.5	5.6	S	Nice coast into **Glenford**
0.5	6.1	L	**SR 204.** Just right in Glenford is a small grocery store
2.0	8.1	R	**CR 64 (Hopewell Indian Road)**
1.8	9.9	S	Cross bridge over Valley Run
2.7	12.6	R	**SR 668**, at stop sign. Immediately encounter big up-then-down hill.
1.6	14.2	S	**CR 78 (Snook Rd.)** SR 668 veers right. This picturesque road is rideable gravel for a mile
1.0	15.2	R	**CR 55 (Mt. Perry Dr.)** at stop sign. Pavement resumes
0.7	15.9	L	**CR 34 (Coopermill Rd.)** at stop sign
1.1	17.0	S	Pass hillside cemetery, on left
0.3	17.3	BR	**CR 67 (Kroft Rd.).** CR 34 bears left
0.9	18.2	L	**TR 108**, near top of hill. *Caution*: Rough, hilly gravel road. If you do ride it, be very careful downhill!
0.9	19.1		**Jacks Hollow Covered Bridge**
0.0	19.1		Backtrack on **TR 108**
0.9	20.0	R	**TR 108 (Kroft Rd.)** at stop sign
1.9	21.9	BL	At stop sign. Road becomes **CR 34**
1.8	23.7	S	Cross over **old iron bridge**
0.1	23.8	R	**SR 204**, at stop sign. *Caution* crossing railroad tracks. You are entering Mt. Perry. On your left is DJ's Market, offering snacks, cold drinks, subs, pizza, and other foods.
0.2	24.0	BR	With **SR 204**. This part of 204 sometimes gets busy. It's hilly at first and then levels out.

Pt.-Pt.	Cume	Turn	Street/Landmark
2.1	26.1	**S**	Cross SR 668
1.8	27.9	**L**	**CR 33 (Bower Rd.)** at farm implement store
0.2	28.1	**L**	To remain on **CR 33**
0.3	28.4	**L**	**CR 51**, at Hopewell Church
0.1	28.5		**Hopewell Church Covered Bridge.** Walk, or use *caution* riding across bridge. After visiting bridge, backtrack to **CR 33**
0.1	28.6	**L**	**CR 33**
1.3	29.9		**Parks/South Covered Bridge**. After visiting bridge, proceed straight on **CR 33**, but be very careful riding through it
1.0	30.9	**R**	**SR 668**. It will be fairly hilly riding toward Somerset
2.5	33.4	**R**	At stop sign. An alluring Dairy Freeze on your left at turn
0.6	34.0		Town square: end of ride. Salute the General!

The Hopewell Church Covered Bridge, spanning Painter Run since 1874.

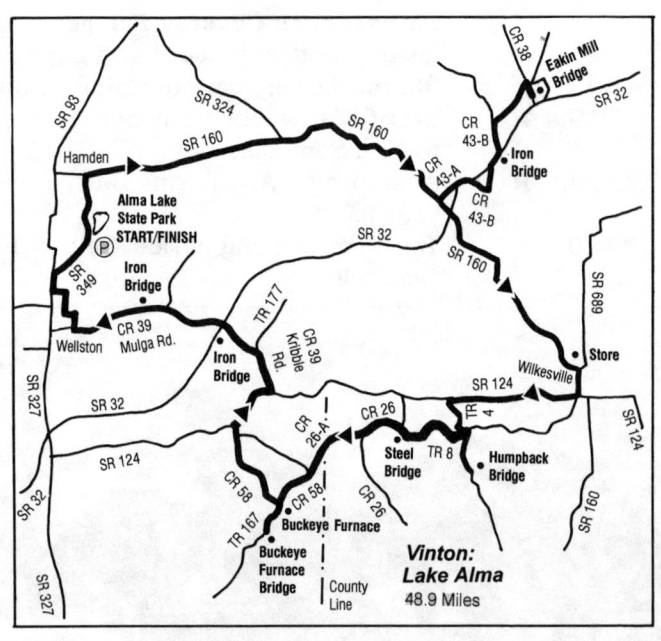

Vinton:
Lake Alma
48.9 Miles

Vinton: Lake Alma—48.9 miles

Terrain: Generally rolling and occasionally flat, with larger hills in the vicinity of the Humpback Bridge in the southern portion of the county.

Road Conditions: Paved and well maintained on the state roads; the backroads are sometimes rough, though, and there are several miles on gravel roads near Humpback Bridge.

Traffic: Moderate on State Route 160, and very light on the other roads.

Points of Interest: Lake Alma State Park; Eakin Mill Covered Bridge; Humpback Covered Bridge; Buckeye Furnace State Memorial; Buckeye Furnace Covered Bridge.

Although the sites on this route are well worth the effort, at the completion of this ride you may feel it is best experienced by car. Firstly, because of the condition of many of the backroads in this part of Vinton County, you spend much of the first half of the ride on a state route (160) that is often devoid of any shoulder. Also, while traffic on State Route 160 is not heavy, a good percentage of it rumbles by in the unpleasant form of coal trucks. Secondly, it is a long ride with demanding hills concentrated where the roads just happen to be the roughest.

With that said, if you must pedal then I guess you will pedal— just give yourself plenty of time and keep your cool on State Route 160. If you ride it on Sunday, traffic should be much more to your liking.

You'll begin this route in the parking lot of **Alma Lake State Park**. Lake Alma is a lovely little lake with a tranquil beach near the parking lot. Certainly, after this ride you'll deserve a refreshing post-ride dip. It also has primitive restrooms, picnic facilities, as well as primitive campsites.

After leaving the state park, you'll ride north on State Route 399, then east on State Route 160, on which you'll spend about 14 miles of this ride. Again, the shoulder disappears and reappears as if by magic; ride it whenever possible. At mile 9.6, you'll get off State Route 160 onto pretty and tranquil backroads that lead you to the **Eakin Mill Covered Bridge.** This bridge is sometimes also called the Aikin's Bridge, Arbaugh Bridge, or Geer Bridge. By way of explanation, Stephen Aiken built a mill near Arbaugh in the early 1930s, and Henry Geer was the miller there for many years. The bridge was built in 1871, the year that Ohio native U.S. Grant was re-elected President. Today, as then, it sits atop the banks of Raccoon Creek. Its road, County Route 38, is now a dead end closed to automotive traffic. That is probably best for this fine old bridge, because it is leaning and in need of repair. It was badly damaged in the early 1970s by trucks used in the construction of nearby State Route 32. There has been talk of repairing it, and hopefully this will happen one day. The bridge may have lost a few boards, but it's lost none of its charm.

After visiting the Eakin Mill/Aikin's/Arbaugh/Geer Covered bridge, you'll backtrack to State Route 160, ride to tiny Wilkesville, then head toward the hilly, gravel, picturesque backroads that lead to the famous **Humpback Covered Bridge**. Built in 1874 to replace a covered bridge on the site burned by arsonists earlier that same year, the Humpback Bridge is one of *only two* examples of humpbacked covered bridges remaining in the U.S. Not only is its back humped, but so is its floor. The unique 174-foot-long bridge (ninth-longest covered bridge in Ohio) with multiple kingpost trusses was built by Martin McGraph and Lyman Wells, contractors from McArthur, for $1,898. It has also been called the Ponn Bridge, for a family who lived nearby, and the Geer's Mill Bridge for the local miller (a brother of the one referenced at the Eakin Mill Bridge), but the obvious, affectionate name of "Humpback" seems destined to stick.

On the day Steve paid a visit to the Humpback Covered Bridge, a sunny June day at the end of record-setting spring rainfalls, Raccoon Creek was swollen and swift. Humpback was soon to be bypassed; the new iron bridge sat next to it, needing only a few finishing touches to ready it for traffic. The creek was not so tranquil as its course, and neither was the wooded, isolated valley that Humpback calls home. A forlorn-appearing gathering sat on lawn chairs or in the back of a pick-up truck parked on the side of the road near the old bridge, watching the water swirl through the partly-submerged branches of recently fallen trees. A 25-year-old man from nearby Wellston apparently had disappeared in the raging waters about a week before. The prevailing assumption was that his drowned body was submerged and tangled in the branches of the fallen trees. It seems these people, friends and acquaintances and a few family members of the missing man, were keeping watch because the local sheriff's department had decided the fast-moving waters were unfit for divers to enter, opting instead to hold out until the water subsided to search for the body. (Steve said this story was later confirmed by a news report on the local radio station.)

The young man who explained the situation said he knew of several drownings along here in recent years. Pointing to a hole in the roof of the bridge on the edge of its northern slope, he said local kids often climb the trusses up to that hole, diving from the roof into the creek below—sometimes with tragic results. Steve left with the young man's words burned into his memory: "Mister, if that bridge could talk, it would tell some real stories."

Over 125 years there would be a lot of stories to tell. Be cautious, and keep that in mind as you pedal off on the hilly, tree-lined road. Keep an eye out for wild turkeys, abundant in the area. Also, pay close attention to the cue sheet directions; these roads swerve and fork frequently, and not only are road signs scarce, but the few that are around are likely to have been twisted around in the wrong direction by local pranksters.

Shortly, you'll enter Jackson County and then reach the **Buckeye Furnace** memorial park and its on-premises covered bridge, appropriately named the **Buckeye Furnace Bridge**. This bridge sits where it was first erected in 1871, over Little Raccoon Creek just west of Buckeye Furnace. It is in relatively good shape and active, and it's safe to assume this bridge will remain that way for many years to come.

The **Buckeye Furnace** was built about 20 years before the bridge (1851), but its practical use ended in 1894. Buckeye Furnace was built during the heyday of the charcoal iron furnace. It was one of about 80 similar furnaces scattered throughout southern Ohio and northern Kentucky known as the "Hanging Rock Iron Region." In producing up to 12 tons of iron per day to feed both the pressing needs of civil war armament and the ravenous industrial revolution, this and other regional iron furnaces stripped the hillsides of trees for furnace fuel and exploited desperate workers eager to earn a living. Employees were often overworked, underpaid, overcharged at the company stores, and little attention was given to their safety on the job.

In the late part of the 19th century, more lucrative ore fields were discovered. Larger iron companies built larger furnaces, taking the iron industry to places like Pittsburgh, where transportation of raw goods and products was easier. Once larger iron plants opened, the Hanging Rock region was unable to keep pace with production and faded into the history books and the surrounding countryside. Today, the massive sandstone-block structure is restored and the nearby area is a nature preserve with hiking trails. On the premises is a replica of the company store which serves as an information and exhibition area. A small admission is charged for the official tour of the furnace and related buildings. (Hours of operation are from Memorial Day to Labor Day, 10 a.m. to 5 p.m.) If you decide against the official tour, you can still take in this impressive structure, free of charge, while visiting the nearby bridge that, unlike the furnace, has not yet outlived its usefulness. There is a shady picnic area near the creek where you can enjoy a snack.

Jackson County is home to two other covered bridges that do not easily lend themselves to the format of this book. Those traveling by car can visit the **Byer Covered Bridge**, at the town of Byer. In the course of researching this book, this bridge had been closed due to very poor conditions. It is located on County Route 31, 0.1 mile west off State Route 327, about 8 miles northwest of Wellston, which is on this route. **Johnson Road Covered Bridge**, which remains active, is in the southwestern corner of the county on TR 291, 0.6 mile east off State Route 776 right where it veers sharply westward toward Pike County.

The roads from Buckeye Furnace to Lake Alma are sometimes rough and hilly, but always paved, usually smooth, and generally not too challenging. You'll pass through the town of Wellston near the end, where you can pick up something cold to drink and/or something to eat, and take it with you to Lake Alma to enjoy after your well-earned swim there.

Directions to the Starting Point: The entrance to Lake Alma State park is on the east side of State Route 349, just north of Wellston in Jackson County, and about a mile south of Hamden and State Route 160 in Vinton County.

Pt.-Pt.	Cume	Turn	Street/Landmark
0.0	0.0	**R**	**SR 349**. Exit parking lot. This state route has light to moderate traffic but no shoulder, so ride carefully.
0.9	0.9	**R**	**SR 160**. The shoulder is fairly wide, but it narrows at times. Ride it, especially on weekdays when coal trucks are rolling.
3.6	4.5	**S**	Shoulder temporarily disappears.
0.6	5.1	**S**	Shoulder reappears.
0.2	5.3	**S**	Junction, **SR 324**. Shoulder disappears.
4.3	9.6	**L**	**CR 43-A** (Sign also states: "Old Route 346")
0.5	10.1	**S**	Steep downhill.
0.4	10.5	**S**	Cross SR 32 at stop sign. This pretty, tree-lined road becomes **43-B**.
0.6	11.1	**S**	**Old iron bridge** on your right.
0.1	11.2	**R**	**SR 32** at stop sign. Ride the shoulder.
0.5	11.7	**L**	**43-B**. Turn with caution! In rainy seasons this road is prone to flooding

Pt.-Pt.	Cume	Turn	Street/Landmark
1.8	13.5	**R**	**CR 38**. There's no sign; just as 43-B curves, look for boulders partially blocking entrance to this dead-end road on your right side.
0.1	13.6		**Eakin Mill Covered Bridge**
0.1	13.7	**L**	Backtrack to **CR 43-B** and turn left. You will now backtrack to **SR 160**.
1.8	15.5	**R**	**SR 32** at stop sign. Ride the shoulder.
0.5	16.0	**L**	**43-B**. Turn with caution!
0.7	16.7	**S**	Cross SR 32 at stop sign. Road becomes **43-A**
0.6	17.3	**S**	Radcliff sign.
0.2	17.5	**L**	**SR 160** at stop sign (T). No shoulder; ride carefully!
0.4	17.9	**S**	Cross SR 32 again, at stop sign.
4.6	22.5	**S**	Junction. **SR 689**. Store on your left.
0.4	22.9	**S**	Enter **Wilkesville**.
0.3	23.2	**R**	**SR 124.**
0.3	23.5	**S**	"Leaving Wilkesville" sign.
0.3	23.8	**S**	Nice downhill coast. The next 2.4 miles are scenic and rolling. The shoulder varies from narrow to nothing, but traffic is generally light to moderate.
2.4	26.2	**L**	**TR 4**, right after steep climb. No sign.
0.3	26.5	**BL**	At fork, to remain on **TR 4**. Paved but rough road.
0.3	26.8	**S**	Gravel (rideable) begins. This pretty road will have moderate hills
0.9	27.7	**S**	Pass straight through crossroads.
0.2	27.9	**BR**	Bear right at curve.
1.1	29.0		**Humpback Covered Bridge**. If, at the time that you visit old Humpback, you are able to ride through it, do so *cautiously*.
0.0	29.0		After visiting bridge, back track on **TR 4**.
1.1	30.1	**BL**	Remain on **TR 4**.
0.3	30.4	**L**	**TR 8**, at crossroads. Rideable gravel under canopy of trees.

Pt.-Pt.	Cume	Turn	Street/Landmark
1.2	31.6	S	Hillside cemetery on left.
0.3	31.9	S	Cross double span steel bridge.
0.2	32.1	R	Still on **TR 8**. Immediate uphill.
0.4	32.5	L	**CR 26**, at stop sign, right after concrete bridge. Curving paved road.
0.9	33.4	BR	**CR 26A (Buckeye Branch Rd.)** at fork.
0.7	34.1	S	**CR 58 (Buckeye Furnace Rd.)** You're now in Jackson County.
1.1	35.2	L	**TR 167 (Buckeye Park Rd.)** Enter **Buckeye Furnace State Memorial Park**
0.5	35.7	S	On your left is the **Buckeye Furnace**.
0.2	35.9	S	On your right is pleasant picnic area by parking lot. Across the street, info/tours available in the **Company Store and Office**.
0.1	36.0	S	**Buckeye Furnace Covered Bridge.** After checking out the bridge, backtrack through park.
0.7	36.7	L	**CR 58 (Buckeye Furnace Rd.)** at stop sign. A rough, paved, flat road.
2.3	39.0	R	**SR 124**
1.3	40.3	L	**CR 39 (Kribble Rd.)** off of bridge. This road gets both rough and hilly.
0.8	41.1	S	On your right is a deep strip-mine coal pit.
0.1	41.2	BL	TR 177 is the right-hand fork; stay on **CR 39** by bearing left.
1.1	42.3	BL	Bear left at fork to cross **iron bridge** and remain on **CR 39.**
0.2	42.5	S	Cross SR 32 at stop sign. Road is still **CR 39** (but now **Mulga Rd.**, too)
1.1	43.6	BL	At fork, to remain on **CR 39**.
0.6	44.2	S	Cross **iron bridge**.
1.6	45.8	S	Straight, after 4-way stop sign. You are entering town of **Wellston**.
0.3	46.1	R	Onto **New York Ave.**, at stop sign.
0.1	46.2	L	Onto **East 9th St.**, at stop sign.

Pt.-Pt.	Cume	Turn	Street/Landmark
0.1	46.3	**R**	Onto **Pennsylvania Ave.** at stop sign. Rax Restaurant on corner to your right. This is the main drag, with a variety of food available.
0.1	46.4	**S**	Traffic light.
0.2	46.6	**S**	Traffic light
0.2	46.8	**S**	Traffic light.
0.2	47.0	**S**	Traffic light.
0.4	47.4	**R**	**SR 349**, just before railroad tracks. Ride shoulder as you are able.
1.1	48.5	**S**	Sign states, "Leaving Jackson Co."
0.4	48.9	**R**	Into **Lake Alma State Park**. Enjoy a swim—this marks the end of this ride.

Vinton County's Humpback Covered Bridge is shown next to the new iron bridge that bypasses it. Built in 1874, the unique 174-foot-long structure is one of only two humpbacked covered bridges remaining in the U.S. Bypassing a bridge allows it to remain in its original setting, but spares it from the rigors of carrying heavy motor vehicle traffic.

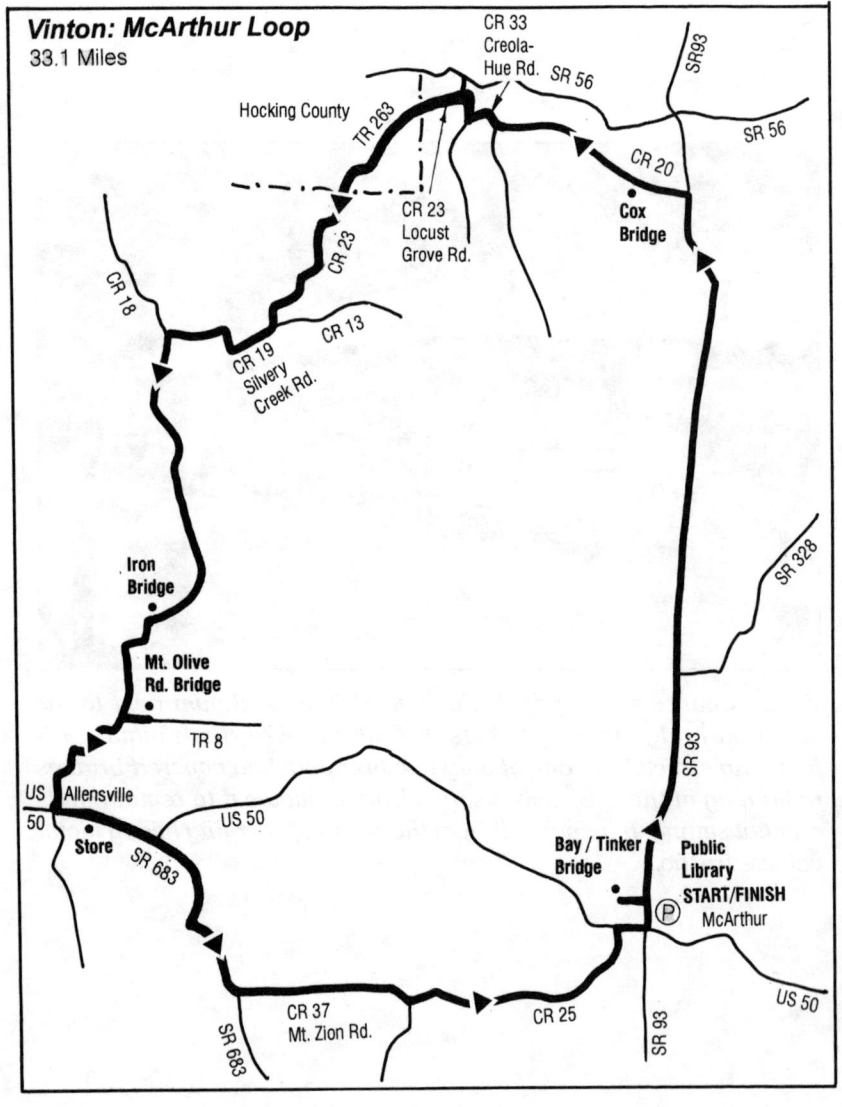

Vinton: McArthur Loop
33.1 Miles

Vinton: McArthur Loop—33.1 miles

Terrain: Primarily rolling, with occasional flat stretches and occasional medium-sized hills, then larger hills the final five miles.

Road Conditions: Generally very good—paved and well maintained.

Traffic: Moderate the first 8 miles on State Route 93 and the 1.3 miles on U.S. 50 later in ride, but both have good, wide shoulders. Otherwise, traffic is quite light and peaceful.

Points of Interest: Bay/Tinker Covered Bridge; Cox Covered Bridge; Mt. Olive Covered Bridge; very scenic backroads with great vistas while in the region of Wayne National Forest.

Vinton County was formed from parts of surrounding counties and named in honor of Ohio Congressman Samuel F. Vinton in 1850. It is almost entirely rural; the starting point of this ride, McArthur, is the county's largest town.

Vinton County and the land that became Vinton County has been served by over 60 covered bridges. Today, five remain, one actively carrying vehicle traffic, one moved and preserved, one closed to traffic but hanging on, and two bypassed for preservation purposes. You will visit three of Vinton County's covered bridges on this ride. On the Vinton-Lake Alma ride, you can visit the other two (as well as one in neighboring Jackson County).

You can park for free anywhere in tranquil downtown McArthur, but this ride starts and ends in the parking lot of the public library. If you ride on Sunday, the one store on this route will be closed, so carry food and drink with you. Riding north out of town on the wide, smooth shoulder of State Route 93, you'll soon reach the Junior Fairgrounds and this ride's first covered bridge, The **Bay** or **Tinker Bridge**.

This 63' bridge was built over Little Raccoon Creek in 1876, the year our nation celebrated its centennial; 90 years later it was moved here, where it presides over a small pond. It had cost well under $1,000 to build the original structure, but about $2,000 to move it to this location. After taking a break at this peaceful locale (peaceful, that is, unless the fair is in town!), you can carefully ride through the bridge and then back to the road via a stone path.

Continuing north on gently rolling State Route 93, you'll soon enter Wayne National Forest territory, through which you'll ride for about the next 20 scenic miles. Shortly after reaching your first true backroad, County Route 20, the bypassed **Cox Bridge** will appear. One of the shortest covered bridges in Ohio, this 40' bridge was built over Brushy Creek (which it still spans) in 1884— a year in which the Ohio Valley was devastated by raging rivers and massive floods. That same year, more tranquil rivers were navigated by adventuring characters in a just-published novel, *Huckleberry Finn.* In late summer, 1992, workers moved the bridge slightly north via a novel method. After jacking up the ends of the bridge and placing metal runners under it, they laid strips of plywood down the banks between it and its new concrete foundations, about 20 feet away. They nailed the plywood strips together and coated them with a layer of heavy grease. Finally, they attached steel cables to the metal runners and, using a front loader on each end, slowly pulled the bridge to its present location.

Continuing on you will encounter tree-lined country roads that offer occasional panoramic vistas. The route takes you through a corner of Hocking County, then re-enters Vinton County heading south toward this route's third and final covered bridge, the **Mt. Olive Road Bridge**. Formerly called the "Grand Staff" bridge, this short (48-foot) structure was built in 1875 by local preacher and Civil War veteran George Washington Pilcher who, besides building at least four Vinton County covered bridges, also built many bridge foundations throughout the area. This tranquil bridge runs over the Mid Fork of Salt Creek. *Use caution when riding across this bridge.*

Riding back toward McArthur, you will encounter a few roller-coaster hills. While they can be fun to ride, a few of them are somewhat demanding. The challenge is worth it as you enter McArthur's town limits riding under a refreshing canopy of shade trees.

Directions to the Starting Point: McArthur is in central Vinton County at the intersection of U.S. 50 and State Route 93. The two roads meet in the center of downtown. Just north of that intersection on State Route 93 (called Market Street in town), on the east side of the street, is the public library, an inconspicuous one-story building. Park either in the parking lot or on the street (unlimited free parking).

Pt.-Pt.	Cume	Turn	Street/Landmark
0.0	0.0	**R**	**Market Street**. This is **SR 93** as you ride north out of town. Take advantage of the smooth, wide shoulder.
1.4	1.4	**L**	Into the **Junior Fairgrounds**. Turn **right** with stone road then **bear right** with it
0.1	1.5		**Bay/Tinker Covered Bridge**. *Use caution riding through it*
0.0	1.5	**S**	Follow stone path on other side of bridge back to **SR 93**
0.1	1.6	**L**	**SR 93**. Continue riding shoulder
6.9	8.5	**L**	**CR 20**. Billboard on left at turn
0.1	8.6		**Cox Covered Bridge**. *Use caution if you ride through it.*
0.0	8.6	**S**	Continue on **CR 20**. A splendid scenic road
2.6	11.2	**BR**	Road becomes **CR 33 (Creola-Hue Rd.)** after stop sign
0.1	11.3	**S**	**Ebenezor Church**, established 1876, and cemetery, on right
0.5	11.8	**L**	**CR 23 (Locust Grove Rd.)** This is a hilly, tree-lined road. In about ¾ mile you'll briefly ride into Hocking County and the road name will temporarily change to **TR 263**, but no signs announce either fact

Pt.-Pt.	Cume	Turn	Street/Landmark
2.2	14.0	S	**CR 23**. A sign indicates you have re-entered Vinton County. The road continues to be simply breathtaking, providing scenic vistas on both sides as you ride atop a ridge
1.9	15.9	S	**CR 19 (Silvery Creek Rd.)** CR 13 veers left
0.1	16.0	R	**CR 19** at country church
1.5	17.5	L	**CR 18**. Big boulder near road in yard directly across from turn
0.6	18.1	S	Big up-then-down hill
1.4	19.5	S	Cross concrete bridge
0.6	20.1	S	Another concrete bridge
0.5	20.6	BR	Immediately after crossing old iron bridge
1.7	22.3	S	Look ahead, left side of road, for next covered bridge
0.2	22.5	L	**TR 8**. Almost immediately, encounter the **Mt. Olive Road Bridge**. When riding across it, *be careful!* After spending time at the bridge, return to **CR 18**
0.1	22.6	L	**CR 18**
1.0	23.6	S	Cross concrete bridge
0.5	24.1	L	**US 50**, at stop sign. This is Allensville (no services—yet). Ride on good shoulder while on US 50
0.7	24.8		Cross-Creek General Store on right— snacks, sandwiches, and 5-cent coffee! Closed Sundays.
0.6	25.4	BR	**SR 683**. No shoulder; exercise caution
2.1	27.5	L	**CR 37 (Mt. Zion Road)**
0.5	28.0	S	Big downhill followed by a bigger uphill over ridge. This will be a roller-coaster ride
1.6	29.6	BL	Road becomes **CR 25**
0.4	30.0	S	Cross concrete bridge
1.9	31.9	S	Pass **McArthur** sign and ride into town

Pt.-Pt.	Cume	Turn	Street/Landmark
0.8	32.7	**R**	**W. Main Street**
0.2	32.9	**L**	**Market Street** at traffic light
0.2	33.1	**R**	**Library** parking. End of route

The Mt. Olive Road Bridge was built in 1875 over the Mid Fork of Salt Creek by George Washington Pilcher. The builder—a preacher and Civil War veteran—built at least four Vinton County bridges and numerous bridge foundations.

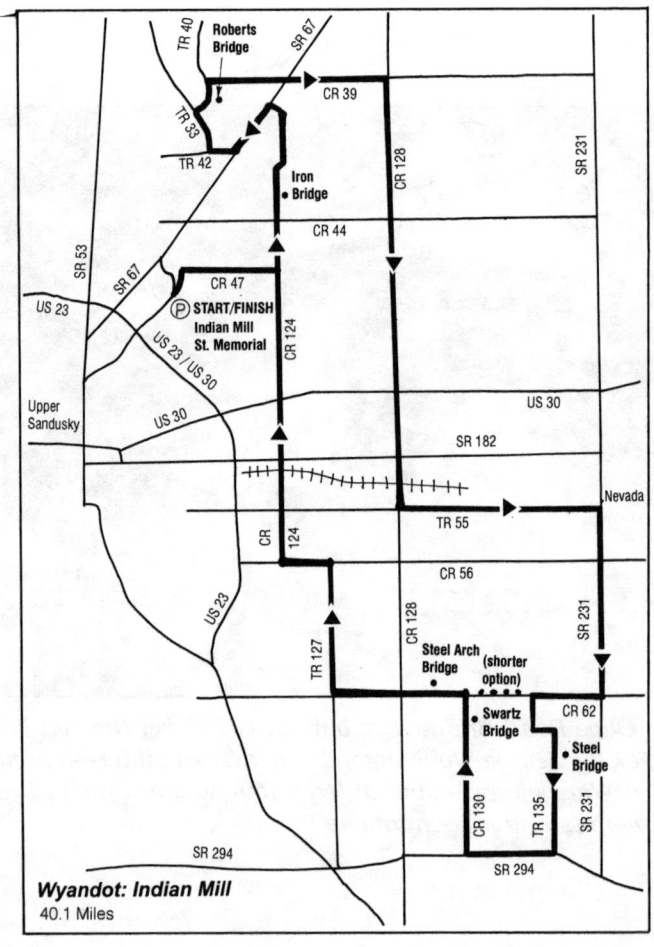

Wyandot: Indian Mill
40.1 Miles

Wyandot: Indian Mill—40.1 miles

Terrain: Mostly flat and occasionally rolling.

Road Conditions: Except for 0.6 miles of rideable gravel, roads are all paved and generally well maintained.

Traffic: Mostly light to nonexistent, with moderate traffic on State Routes 67 and 231, both with good shoulders.

Points of Interest: Indian Mill State Memorial; Chief Tarhe Monument; Parker Covered Bridge; Swartz Covered Bridge; old iron bridges; Red-brick one-room schoolhouses; old country churches; smooth, tranquil roads through wooded farmlands.

Named for the Wyandot Indians who once controlled the region that is now Ohio and made their headquarters here, Wyandot County is an arrowhead hunter's paradise. It's not bad for cyclists, either! The roads are mostly paved and smooth, with little traffic and lots of roadside trees, farmlands, and historic structures.

Wyandot County has seen at least 20 covered bridges; today, two remain to carry traffic, both built with Howe trusses in the 1870s. You will visit both bridges during this ride. The tour begins near one historic structure, the **Indian Mill**. The mill, built in 1861, got its name from another mill that once stood 300 feet upstream. It was built by the U.S. government as a token of appreciation to local Wyandot Indians who remained loyal during the War of 1812. This mill is unique in that it utilizes covered-bridge type construction.

The old mill now houses the nation's first museum about the history of milling. If you take this ride on a Friday, Saturday, or Sunday, from June to October, you might want to cross the old iron bridge (from the parking lot starting/ending point) and stop by the museum (admission is $1.00). Either way, the old iron bridge is still worth a look. Built in 1914, the iron bridge replaced a covered bridge that was lost in the great flood of 1913. A crowd of locals reportedly gathered nearby to watch as the rising, raging river slowly consumed the covered bridge. In the parking area is another old iron bridge built in 1891 and later moved here for use as a footbridge. Also here are shaded picnic tables overlooking the Sandusky River, which crosses under both of this ride's covered bridges. Designated a state scenic river, it takes its name from the Wyandot word (pronounced "San-doo-stee") meaning "Water within pools."

Leaving the parking lot, you'll ride over smooth flat roads, soon encountering the interesting **Chief Tarhe Monument**. Wyandot Chief Tarhe earned the wampum belt of peace, given him by General "Mad" Anthony Wayne at the signing of the Treaty of Greenville in 1795. Later, he refused to take part in the uprising led by Tecumseh in southern Ohio, then joined with local tribes to assist U.S. forces during the War of 1812. Stop and read the inscription on the roadside memorial marker. Several miles northwest of this spot, Colonel William Crawford, the namesake of the county just east of Wyandot County, was burned at the stake in the far less peaceful year of 1782.

Not far from the monument is the **Roberts Bridge**, constructed in 1873. At 172 feet long, the Roberts Bridge—along with Brown County's Bowman/Eagle Creek Bridge—is the longest single-span covered bridge in Ohio. As you can read on the plaque outside the bridge, arsonists nearly destroyed it in May, 1991, burning one-third of its span. Immediate salvage action by the county kept the bridge from falling into the river. The Cross Over The Bridge Again Committee was formed to continue and expand the fund-raising efforts started by the county historical society. In the end, the bridge was saved thanks to the efforts of many devoted people, and in 1992 it was rebuilt.

Notice the bricks at both ends of the bridge, inscribed with the names of those who helped with the restoration effort and expenses. Today it is once again a sturdy, serene structure that some have called "The Peace Bridge."

Next you will cover mostly flat farmland, touch the tiny town of Nevada (food is available there), then begin to encounter rolling hills and old one-room schoolhouses, finally reaching the **Swartz Bridge**, built in 1878. By the 1980s and early 90s, its interior was coated with colorful graffiti, which—believe it or not—may have helped preserve it. The roof was badly deteriorated, and in late 1992, with funding from The Cross Over The Bridge Again Committee, the roof was restored. Eventually the graffiti was removed and the bridge was repainted barn red.

The river meanders nicely through a meadow to cross under the bridge, which has seen many picnics in days gone by. The Delaware Indians had a village and council house about a mile from the bridge site. Several fine old country churches also lie along the route. If these interest you, they all have cemeteries that include the headstones of Civil War veterans.

Directions to the Starting Point: The Indian Mill State Memorial parking lot is right across the big old iron bridge from Indian Mill on County Road 47, 1 mile east of State Route 67, 2.5 miles northeast of Upper Sandusky.

Pt.-Pt.	Cume	Turn	Street/Landmark
0.0	0.0	**R**	Exit **Indian Mill** parking lot by turning right onto **CR 47**
1.7	1.7	**L**	**CR 124** (T)
0.8	2.5	**S**	Stop sign. Cross CR 44
0.3	2.8	**S**	Old **iron bridge**; private lake on left.
0.7	3.5	**BL**	Fork in road; stay on **CR 124**!
0.8	4.3	**L**	**SR 67** (T). Ride on shoulder
0.5	4.8	**S**	**Smithville** (Not on any map)
0.5	5.3	**R**	**TR 42**. At intersection, **old church** (1888) with cemetery.
0.3	5.6	**R**	**TR 37**
0.3	5.9	**S**	On left, roadside **memorial marker** for Wyandot Chief Tarhe.
0.4	6.3	**R**	**TR 40**.
0.2	6.5	**S**	**Roberts Covered Bridge**

Pt.-Pt.	Cume	Turn	Street/Landmark
0.3	6.8	**R**	**CR 39** (road sign on left)
1.2	8.0	**S**	Stop sign. Cross **SR 67**
1.7	9.7	**R**	**CR 128**. *Caution*: sharp drop-off at road-edge
1.0	10.7	**S**	Stop sign. Check out the converted **brick schoolhouse** across road
1.0	11.7	**S**	Stop sign. **Old church** on right
2.5	14.2	**S**	Stop sign. *Caution* crossing US 30.
1.0	15.2	**S**	Stop sign. Cross SR 182
0.4	15.6	**S**	Railroad tracks. *Use caution!*
0.4	16.0	**L**	**TR 55**, at the stop sign
2.1	18.1	**S**	Check out the country spread on the right!
0.8	18.9	**S**	Stop sign. On your left is **Nevada Consolidated School**, built in 1876.
0.1	19.0	**S**	Stop sign
0.1	19.1	**R**	**SR 231**, at the stop sign. Ride on the shoulder. If you need refreshments or a bite to eat, visit sleepy downtown **Nevada**, several blocks to your left.
2.8	21.9	**R**	**CR 62**
1.0	22.9	**L**	**TR 135**. [*Option:* to cut 4.9 miles from this ride, proceed 1.0 mile **straight** on **CR 62** then turn **left** on **CR 130**, and proceed 0.2 mile to rejoin route at the **Swartz Bridge**]
0.5	23.4	**SL**	Road turns sharply left
0.3	23.7	**SR**	Road turns sharply right
0.5	24.2	**S**	**Old steel bridge** high above the Sandusky River (great fishing spot!)
1.0	25.2	**S**	On left, **old one-room schoolhouse**
0.3	25.5	**R**	**SR 294** (T)
1.3	26.8	**R**	**CR 130**. Covered Bridge sign just before turn. On left as you turn is **old schoolhouse** blanketed with vegetation
2.2	29.0	**S**	**Swartz Covered Bridge**. *Caution:* Walk, do not ride, across bridge

Pt.-Pt.	Cume	Turn	Street/Landmark
0.2	29.2	**L**	**CR 62** (T)
0.2	29.4	**S**	Old steel arch bridge over Brokensword Creek (Named by local Indians after they captured Colonel William Crawford, who broke his sword over rocks on the creek bank so it would not be used against him. It wasn't—they burned him at the stake instead!)
0.9	30.3	**S**	Stop sign. Cross CR 128
1.0	31.3	**R**	**TR 127**
1.0	32.3	**S**	Stop sign. Across road on right is **old church**, established 1852.
0.2	32.5	**S**	Another **old schoolhouse** on left, built in 1885
0.8	33.3	**L**	**CR 56**
0.8	34.1	**R**	**TR 124**
0.1	34.2	**S**	Gravel stretch (not bad) begins
0.6	34.8	**S**	Stop sign. Pavement resumes
0.4	35.2	**S**	**Old church** on left
0.1	35.3	**S**	*Use care* crossing railroad tracks
0.3	35.6	**S**	Stop sign. Cross SR 182
0.9	36.5	**S**	Stop sign. *Exercise extreme caution* crossing US 30! Road becomes **CR 124** after you cross
1.8	38.3	**L**	**CR 47**
1.8	40.1	**L**	Into **Indian Mill** parking lot. End of route.

The Benetka Road Covered Bridge, circa 1900, traverses the Ashtabula River. The 115-foot Town Lattice structure was renovated in 1985 with the addition of a laminated arch that runs the entire length of the bridge.

Glossary of Bridge Terms, Including Truss Types

Abutment: The bridge foundation on the opposing banks. These are typically made from limestone or sandstone (often quarried nearby), bedrock, or concrete. (*see also: Pier*).

Arch: Curved timbers used to strengthen standard truss designs. (*see: Burr Truss*).

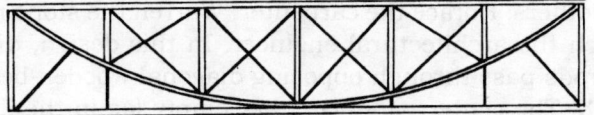

BOWSTRING SUSPENSION TRUSS

Bowstring Suspension Truss: As shown in the illustration, this design utilizes intermediate wood members attached to steel eye-bars (solid lines), crisscrossing steel rods (solid lines), and, most significantly, an inverted steel bowstring (the line curving the length of the illustration). In this design, the floor beams are suspended from steel stirrups hanging down from the wooden vertical/eye-bar intersection. Only two exist in the world, and one is included in this *RIDE GUIDE*: The John Bright #2 Bridge in Fairfield County.

Brace: Diagonal timbers slanted toward the center of the truss.

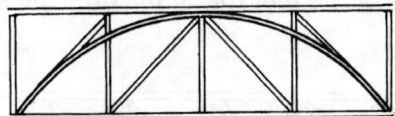

BURR TRUSS

Burr Truss: This design was patented by prolific bridge builder Theodore Burr in 1804. In his patent, he claimed only the wooden arch. The arch can be used in combination with any truss, but it is most typically used with a multiple kingpost truss on bridges over 50' in length. Sometimes the arch is built both inside and outside of its truss, making a "double arch." The arch ends are fitted into the face of the bridge's abutments. In this book, bridges identified as having arches have the Burr arch design or some facsimile of same. Nearly 300 covered bridges in the U.S. have Burr arches.

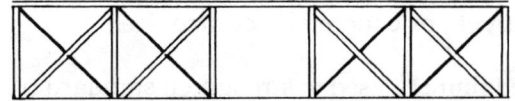

CHILD'S
TRUSS

Child's Truss: The Child's truss design comes from the three Childs brothers: Horace the carpenter, Warren the stone mason, and Enoch the architectural engineer. In this design, diagonal steel tie-rods pass through opposing diagonal wooden beams to form an X. The center panel is either empty (as in the illustration) or with a kingpost. In the illustration, the solid lines represent the tie-rods. Less than 10 of these remain in the country.

Chord: Upper and lower chords are the horizontal timbers that encase, respectively, the top and bottom ends of the truss timbers.

Compression Members: The diagonal truss beams that squeeze with the pressure of a crossing load.

Counter Brace: The diagonal truss timbers that point away from the center of the truss.

Eaves: The edges of the roof that hang over the sides of the covered bridge.

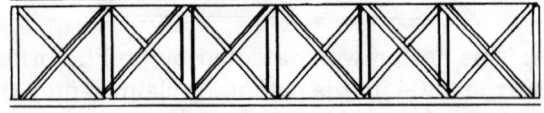

HOWE
TRUSS

Howe Truss: Patented in 1840 by Massachusetts native William Howe, the Howe Truss (like the Long Truss) consists of beams forming Xs, with one leg of each beam a double-beam encasing the other leg. Instead of vertical wooden posts between the Xs, this design uses iron tie-rods (the solid vertical lines in the illustration) that can be adjusted with turnbuckles. This design granted superior strength and durability to all-wood designs and was the forerunner of the iron bridge designs to come. Over 100 Howe Truss bridges remain nationwide.

KINGPOST TRUSS

Kingpost Truss: The Kingpost is the oldest, most basic truss design. With two diagonals and the central "kingpost" it forms two load-absorbing right triangles. Formerly built beneath the roadway, it became commonly built above the roadway when it was discovered that it worked just as well there. Plus, this way it would no longer serve as an unintentional dam in the case of high waters! In this simple design, the slanting diagonal timbers serve as compression members and the kingpost timber is the tension member. As 25' to 30' is about the maximum length for a simple kingpost bridge, there are relatively few of them (*see also: Multiple Kingpost Truss*).

Laminated Arch: Multiple planks that are bolted together into an arch, sometimes used instead of a single, solid beam.

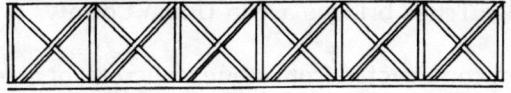

LONG TRUSS

Long Truss: Patented by designer/promoter (as opposed to builder) Stephen Long, this design consists of boxed panels with diagonal beams forming an X within each panel. One of the legs in each X is a double beam that encases the other leg. This design was used most extensively in the 1830s and 1840s. Today, less than 30 remain in the U.S.

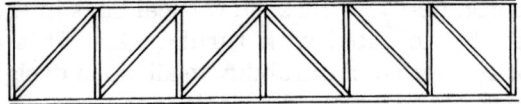

MULTIPLE KINGPOST

Multiple Kingpost Truss: The multiple kingpost utilizes any number of diagonal beams, all slanting toward the truss center and all forming right triangles. This allows for a longer span than a simple kingpost, up to around 100'. Sometimes, the multiple kingpost was built with a center panel that was either left empty (as a simple square) or else framed two diagonal beams forming an X.

Panel: Panels are the individual sections of a truss that are separated by vertical timbers.

PARTRIDGE TRUSS

Partridge Truss: This interesting truss design was patented as the "High Bridge Truss Improvement" by Reuben Partridge in 1872. As shown in the illustration, this design uses a combination of crisscrossing triple and double diagonal beams; strategically placed iron rods (solid lines) have been added later, and are not original. Besides Franklin County's Bergstresser Bridge, all surviving Partridge Truss bridges are in Union County.

Pier: A foundation constructed from stone, concrete, or steel that supports the center of a bridge. A long bridge may have more than one pier. (*see also: Abutment*).

Portal: The entrances at either end of a covered bridge, including the surrounding wood that protects the ends of the bridge's interior.

Post: The vertical timbers of a truss.

PRATT TRUSS

Pratt Truss: Patented by Thomas Pratt in 1844, the Pratt design was originally all wood, but as iron and steel became readily available, iron rods replaced the diagonal wood beams. This was the preferred form of Pratt Truss covered bridges. The vertical planks are three-deep, with two parallel diagonal iron rods between each. There are only five or six Pratt Truss Bridges remaining in the country, and only two in Ohio—two new ones in Ashtabula County.

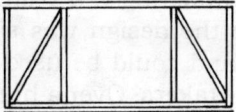

QUEEN POST TRUSS

Queenpost Truss: The queenpost truss is an alteration of the basic kingpost truss that allowed for a longer span, generally up to 60' or 70'. Instead of the one vertical member at its center, queenposts have two that are separated/attached by a horizontal beam up top, as in the illustration. This leaves an open panel in the center.

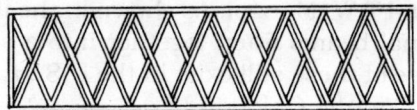

SMITH TRUSS

Smith Truss: Patented by Ohio native Robert Smith, founder of the prolific Smith Bridge Company, the typical Smith Truss bridge is over 100' long. This design consists of opposing diagonal beams forming Xs the length of the bridge. No center panel is used. The Smith Truss was sometimes built using one double diagonal encasing one single diagonal in each X panel, as shown in the illustration. About 20 Smith Truss bridges still exist.

Span: A bridge's length from abutment to abutment. A single pier makes a two-span bridge; two piers make for a three-span bridge.

Tension member: A bridge's vertical posts that get pulled downward by crossing loads.

TOWN TRUSS

Town Truss: This lattice truss design was patented by Ithiel Town in 1820. The crisscrossing planks shown in the illustration are fastened together by wooden nails called "tree pins." Not a builder, Town traveled the country promoting and selling the rights to his new truss design. Because the design was simple, strong, required minimal materials, and could be used on bridges up to 200' long, Town found many takers. Over a hundred still exist in the U.S.

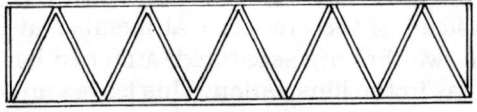

WARREN TRUSS

Warren Truss: The simple Warren Truss was patented in 1838 by James Warren and T.W. Morzini. As shown in the illustration, it consists of diagonal beams fitted together into a series of inverted Vs. Only three of these still exist in the U.S., two of which are in Montgomery County, Ohio.

Basic Data on Bridges

Below is the basic data for most of the covered bridges in Ohio. Listed in column one are the bridges grouped by county. An asterisk beside the bridge name indicates that the structure is listed on the National Register of Historic Places.

The second column has the bridge's official number designations—the first two digits (35) identify the state (Ohio), the second two digits the county, and the third two digits the bridge. These numbers have been established because many bridges have more than one name, and some names have more than one bridge; always use the number when corresponding about a bridge.

The third column lists the date built, if known. The fourth column has the bridge's length. In the fifth column is the bridge's truss type (MKP= multiple kingpost). See the Glossary, beginning on page 93, for descriptions of the various truss types.

Bridge	I.D. #	Date	Length	Truss Type
Ashtabula County				
Dewey Road	35-04-03	1873	115'	Town
Creek Road	35-04-05	——	112'	Town
Middle Road	35-04-06	1868	136'	Howe
Root Road	35-04-09	1868	97'	Town
Benetka Road	35-04-12	c1900	115'	Town+Arch
Graham Road	35-04-13	1867	85'	Town
South Denmark Road	35-04-14	1868	80'	Town
Doyle Road	35-04-16	1876	84'	Town
Mechanicsville	35-04-18	1867	154'	Howe
Harpersfield*	35-04-19	1868	234'	2-span Howe
Riverdale Road	35-04-22	1874	120'	Town
Warner Hollow*	35-04-25	1867	120'	3-span Town
State Road	35-04-58	1983	157'	2-span Town
Caine Road	35-04-61	1986	96'	Pratt
Giddings Road	35-04-62	1995	104'	Pratt
Netcher Road	35-04-63	1999	110'	Haupt + Arch

Bridge	**I.D. #**	**Date**	**Length**	**Truss Type**
Athens County				
Palos*	35-05-01	1875	75'	MKP
Kidwell*	35-05-02	1880	96'	Howe
Brown County				
Brown	35-08-04	1878	129'	Smith
New Hope	35-08-05	1878	170'	Howe+Arch
McCafferty	35-08-08	1870	157'	Howe
Bowman/				
Eagle Creek*	35-08-18	1875	172'	Smith
North Pole Rd.	35-08-23	1875	156'	Smith
George Miller	35-08-34	1878	154'	Smith
Columbiana County				
McClellan	35-15-02	1871	53'	MKP
Teegarden	35-15-05	1876	66'	MKP
Church Hill Rd*	35-15-08	1870	22'	KP
Thomas Malone	35-15-96	1870	42'	MKP
Sells	35-15-01	1878/ 1994	50'	MKP
Fairfield County				
Hizey	35-23-07	1891	83'	MQP+Arch
John Bright #2	35-23-10	1881	75'	Susp.+Arch
Hannaway	35-23-15	1901	86'	MKP
Johnson	35-23-16	1887	98'	Howe
Zeller-Smith	35-23-19	1891	79'	MKP
McLeery	35-23-25	1864	52'	MKP
Charles Holliday	35-23-30	1897	98'	MKP
R.F.Baker	35-23-33	1871	66'	MKP
Hartman	35-23-38	1888	48'	Queen
Mink Hollow	35-23-43	1887	51'	MKP
Rock Mill*	35-23-48	1901	37'	Queen
Franklin County				
Bergstresser*	35-25-03	1887	125'	Partridge
Greene County				
Cemetery Road	35-29-01	1886	60'	Howe
West Engle				
Mill Road	35-29-03	1877	135'	Smith
Stevenson Rd.	35-29-15	1877	95'	Smith
Charlton Mill	35-29-16	1883	119'	Howe
Ballard Road	35-29-18	1883	80'	Howe

Bridge	I.D. #	Date	Length	Truss Type
Guernsey County				
Indian Camp	35-30-04	—	36'	MKP
Armstrong	35-30-12	c1849	76'	MKP
Jackson County				
Buckeye Furnace	35-40-11	1871	59'	Smith
Licking County				
Boy Scout Camp	35-45-04	—	49'	MKP
Shoults/				
Girl Scout	35-45-05	1879	68'	MKP
Gregg	35-45-06	1881	124'	MKP
Davis Farm	35-45-25	1947	50'	MKP
Logan County				
McColly*	35-46-01	1876	125'	Howe
Bickham	35-46-03	1877	94'	Howe
Monroe County				
Foraker*	35-56-14	1886	92'	MKP
Long/Knowlton	35-56-18	1887	192'	MKP+Arch
Montgomery County				
Germantown*	35-57-01	1865	100'	Susp.+Truss
Feedwire Road	35-57-03	1870	42'	Warren+Arch
Jasper Road/				
Mud Lick	35-57-36	1869	50'	Warren+Arch
Morgan County				
Barkhurst Mill	35-58-15	1872	81'	MKP+Arch
Rosseau	35-58-32	—	58'	MKP
Helmick Mill	35-58-35	1867	74'	MKP
Adams/				
San Toy	35-58-38	1875	58'	MKP
Noble County				
Manchester	35-61-33	1915	49'	MKP
Parrish	35-61-34	1914	81'	MKP
Park Hill	35-61-40	—	44'	MKP

Bridge	I.D. #	Date	Length	Truss Type
Perry County				
Parks/South*	35-64-02	1883	58'	MKP
Hopewell Church	35-64-03	1874	55'	MKP
Jacks Hollow	35-64-05	1879	60'	MKP
Preble County				
Harshman*	35-68-03	1894	104'	Childs
Dixon Branch	35-68-04	1887	50'	Childs
Roberts	35-68-05	1829	79'	DRB
Brubaker*	35-68-06	1887	85'	Childs
Christman*	35-68-12	1895	92'	Childs
Geeting*	35-68-12	1895	92'	Childs
Warnke*	35-68-14	1895	52'	Childs
Union County				
Upper Darby	35-80- 01	1868	94'	Partridge
Spain Creek	35-80-02	c1870	64'	Partridge
Treacle Creek	35-80-03	1868	94'	Partridge
Little Darby	35-80-04	1873	102'	Partridge
Vinton County				
Mt.Olive*	35-82-04	1875	48'	Queen
Bay/Tinker	35-82-05	1876	63'	MKP
Humpback/ Geer Mill*	35-82-06	1874	165'	MKP+Arch
Eakin Mill/ Arbaugh	35-82-07	1871	111'	MKP+Arch
Cox	35-82-10	1884	40'	Queen
Washington County				
Shinn*	35-84-03	1886	98'	MKP+Arch
Henry	35-84-06	1894	45'	MKP
Root*	35-84-04	1878	65'	Long
Harra*	35-84-11	1878	95'	Long
Bell	35-84-12	1888	63'	MKP
Mill Branch	35-84-17	1885	59'	MKP
Hills/Hildreth*	35-84-24	1878	122'	Howe
Hune*	35-84-27	1879	128'	Long
Rinard*	35-84-28	1876	130'	Smith

Bridge	I.D. #	Date	Length	Truss Type
Wyandot County				
Parker*	35-88-03	1873	172'	Howe
Swartz	35-88-05	1878	96'	Howe

Note: The Humpback Geer Mill CB is a Three-span MKP with arch. The Eakin Mill/Arbaugh CB is a double MKP with arch.

The Mechanicsville Road Covered Bridge in Ashtabula County is closed to vehicular traffic as it awaits restoration. Built in 1867, the 154-foot bridge is the oldest in the county.

You can visit the Buckeye Furnace Bridge in Jackson County while taking the Vinton-Lake Alma ride on page 71. It was erected over Little Raccoon Creek in 1871 and is still active.

County Tourist Bureaus & Chambers of Commerce

The State of Ohio Travel Hotline can be reached at:
1-800-BUCKEYE

Ashtabula County
Convention and Visitors Bureau
1850 Austinburg Road
Austinburg, Ohio 44010
440-275-3202

Athens County
Convention and Visitors Bureau
667 East State Street
Athens, Ohio 45701
1-800-878-9767

Fairfield County
Visitors and Convention Bureau
P.O. Box 2450
Lancaster, Ohio 43130
1-800-626-1296

Franklin County
Greater Columbus Convention & Visitors Bureau
90 North High Street
Columbus, Ohio 43215
1-800-345-4FUN

Perry County
Development/Tourism Center
120 West Brown Street
New Lexington, Ohio 43764
1-800-343-7379

Preble County
Eaton/Preble County Chamber of Commerce
Eaton National Bank Building
P.O. Box 303
Eaton, Ohio 45320-0303

Vinton County
Chamber of Commerce
P.O. Box 14
McArthur, Ohio 45651
740-596-5033

Wyandot County
Visitors & Convention Bureau
P.O. Box 357
Upper Sandusky, Ohio 43351
419-294-3349

References

The authors would like to acknowledge the following books, which were very helpful in assembling the historical and anecdotal information on the covered bridges and other points of interest covered in this *RIDE GUIDE*:

Ohio Historic Bridge Guide, published by the Ohio Historic Bridge Association, Columbus, Ohio

The Covered Bridges of Ohio: An Atlas and History, by Miriam Wood. Old Trail Printing Company, 1993

Covered Bridges on the Byways of Ohio, by Bryan Ketcham

Covered Bridges Today, by Brenda Krekler

Particular Places, by Marcy Hawley. Orange Frazer Press, 1993

Natural Acts, by Stephen Ostrander

Ohio: Off the Beaten Path, by George Zimmermann. Globe Pequot Press, 1998

Travel Historic Ohio, by Nancy Hochstetter. Guide Press, 1986

Life in the Slow Lane, by Jeff Traylor